CARSPOTTING

CARSPOTTING

The Real Adventures of Irvine Welsh

Sandy Macnair

BLACK & WHITE PUBLISHING

First published 2011
by Black & White Publishing Ltd
29 Ocean Drive, Edinburgh EH6 6JL

1 3 5 7 9 10 8 6 4 2   11 12 13 14

ISBN: 978 1 84502 368 3

Typeset by Iolaire Typesetting, Newtonmore
Printed and bound by MPG Books Ltd, Bodmin

CONTENTS

Acknowledgements

Sincere thank yous are due to several good people who contributed towards the publication of this book.

The staff at Black & White Publishing and Campbell Brown in particular offered invaluable support and good advice and without their input this book would have been unlikely to see the light of day. Dealing with someone who is a self-confessed technological numpty of monumental proportions cannot have been easy for them or others who assisted in converting numerous pages of handwritten scrawl into the finished article. So, thanks here are mainly due to David Todd, whose endless patience extended to taking frantic phone calls in the early hours of the morning after I actually acquired a laptop ("Help! What button do I press? The text has vanished!"), with general good humour. Before that, Jeni Jones, Stu Jones, Hannah Blackshaw and Kim Livingstone all aided and abetted in helping me avoid the horrors of modern technology one way or another. Take a bow, folks. A tip of my trilby is also due to Ted Brack, who also offered encouragement and helpful advice from an early stage. Ta, Ted.

Last and not least I must thank the subject himself – Irvine Welsh. Many people might have baulked at having their dodgy escapades from the past dragged into the cruel, harsh daylight many years later but he was happy to pass the content of this book virtually unaltered. So cheers to you too, old pal!

Sandy Macnair

HEALTH WARNING
How to use this book safely

Please note the symbols displayed on the opening pages of each chapter. These indicate how many pints you may drink before finishing the book, at the rate of one pint per chapter.

In accordance with Government guidelines, we recommend the following timescale:

Heavy drinkers take 2–4 days
Moderate drinkers take 5–7 days
Light drinkers up to a fortnight
Teetotallers put this book back on the shelf right now!
 It ain't for you!

WARNING
It is dangerous to exceed the recommended dose

INTRO...

It was the Best of times, it was the cursed of times. George of that ilk was strutting his stuff at Easter Road but Hibs were still heading for relegation. As the 1970s drew to a close, Irvine Welsh and I were there on the terraces, thinking about quitting our terrible jobs in the Civil Service. We had no discernible ambitions of any sort – apart from an over-riding ambition to escape from the stultifying confines of the General Register Office. Well, that's not *quite* true . . .

When Irvine's boss found him bleary-eyed, unshaven and smelling of drink at his desk one morning, he rounded on him despairingly. "Irvine! Have you *no* ambitions whatsoever?"

"Yes," replied Welsh in all seriousness. "I want to be a messenger."

"*A messenger?*" barked the boss. "What kind of an ambition is that? So you want to end up as a walking vegetable, do you?"

"Well, it beats ending up as a desk-bound vegetable," retorted Irv.

"Oh yes? Really? So you'd rather be on your feet all day? I don't think so!" replied his Executive Officer sarcastically.

Irvine duly stood up and proceeded to spend the rest of the day on his feet, albeit still behind his desk, sulkily going about his paperwork. The boss-man just retreated in abject defeat.

So, Irvine's back might have been killing him but he *had* proved his point. But what *was* the point exactly? There was no point in anything as far as we could see – but so what? At least back in those far-off, pre-Thatcher days, you could simply jack in any job you didn't like because you could always get another one. That happy situation would soon change irrevocably, however.

INTRO...

Finally, we did quit our jobs and went looking for . . . what? Excitement? We weren't gonna find that watching this Hibs team, sadly. The world was our oyster but so too was the West End Oyster Bar. That notwithstanding, the book you are now holding in your hot little hands documents where it all began – if "it" refers to a thirty-year-long insane odyssey involving ugly confrontations with Hearts supporters, jellied eels, motorcycle gangs, deranged Buddhists, smacked-out hookers, oddly coloured sheep, gin-soaked lesbians and police officers. Loads and loadsy polis, likesay.

I hope you find the following story as gruelling to read as I did actually living it. Do enjoy!

Sandy Macnair

BLUE RAM BLUES

Spectral horses, azure sheep

The Filth . . . and the fury

Vertigo terror in York

Strange blobs in the sky

I stumbled along the Portobello foreshore in the savage early morning light, explosions reverberating around my aching skull. The monotonous rumble of traffic sounded more like heavy bombers inside my head. Shuddering and shaking, I picked my way gingerly through Musselburgh, towards the roundabout at the east side of the town where I was due to meet Welsh. I bitterly regretted it now, of course, but it was too late. Sinister jolts of reality from the previous evening's events began to crackle through my brain, as I beheld my compatriot up ahead. Holy Christ! I stopped abruptly, as I suddenly also saw myself, being deposited at my front door by the occupants of a panda car . . . I shut my eyes tightly but the unwelcome images continued to flow. Vomit, shattered bus shelters, police officers . . .

Irvine, for once fairly bright-eyed and bushy-tailed at such an hour, looked at me disapprovingly. It was obvious from my general demeanour that all was not well.

"Well?"

Did he mean as in "not ill" or as in "what the fuck happened to you last night?" I wondered. A bit of both perhaps.

"I . . . I got arrested . . . in Oxgangs . . ." I explained rather uncertainly.

"What?"

I repeated the known facts; namely that an arrest had occurred in

3

the Oxgangs area of the city of Edinburgh sometime between the hours of 12 midnight and 4 a.m., but what exactly for, I could not say. Although by this time I'd actually remembered why they'd driven me home. A police officer had angrily yelled that he wasn't going to dirty his nice clean cells by placing *me* in them, but I decided not to mention this. Irvine shook his head sadly at the irresponsible folly of his old acquaintance. I thought his scandalised reaction was a bit rich but his manner changed noticeably when I, in turn, demanded an explanation. Where, I wanted to know, were we going and why?

"Grantham," he said decisively.

"Where the hell is that?"

"Dunno really. About 300 miles south somewhere . . . I think."

"Why?" was the next obvious question.

He looked at me awkwardly for a moment, before allowing his gaze to drift off towards the horizon.

"I've got to make a court appearance there," he admitted.

Heartfelt regret at my foolishness in agreeing to accompany him increased rapidly as the morning wore on. But *why* had I agreed to it? Like most things, you could put it down to drink. That warm glow of friendship that permeates your whole being after about the sixth pint of an evening, when your so-called "friend" casually mentions his yearning for a travelling companion on a journey he is due to take. "I'll be there for you, good buddy!" you respond loyally – if you ever knew the reason for the trip in the first place, you've certainly forgotten it after the eighth pint.

After two hours of fruitless thumb flapping, we caught a bus as far as Dunbar to spur us on our way, and the heat on that hellish vehicle only intensified my condition of extreme dehydration and general ill-health. Medicine in the form of two full sized bottles of Irn Bru failed to do the trick. Its manufacturer's boast of it being "Made In Scotland – From Girders". That may well be true but I just felt as if the girders in question were slowly being applied with increasing pressure to each side of my broiling brain. Pins and needles ran up and down my body as the sweat lashed down my chalk-white face. Of course, this display of abject misery cheered Irvine up no end. He flung his head back and laughed delightedly at each tremor that galvanised my dilapidated carcass.

At Dunbar we set off on foot again. The omens were not good. There comes a point in every hitchhiker's career when he realises that today is simply not going to be his day. It's as if the entire motoring classes of Western Europe have been to view Rutger Hauer in *The Hitcher* at their local fleapit the night before and think "Oh no – no way!" when men with flapping fingers swim into focus at the roadside.

In any case, a hitcher has to look the part.

"Would I stop for me?" I was forced to ask myself, before answering resoundingly in the negative. Ragged and red-eyed is all very well if you're tramping about in the far north bearing a rucksack the size of Aviemore and exuding an air of "Bona-fide traveller" to the wary motorist. The lack of a rucksack was probably our major mistake. It's always wise to carry one – even if it's empty – to supplement the overall image.

A few piddling little lifts conveyed us through the Borders but after getting stuck outside the bizarre looking *Cat Inn* near Scremerston for ages, we realised that other methods would have to be implemented. We stopped a bus, paid the fare as far as Alnwick, but neglected to get off until it reached Newcastle. A change of driver en route enabled us to get away with it and, briefly buoyed up, we rashly blew some of our meagre funds on a slap-up Chinese meal.

It has to be said that even in my very dodgy state, I knew that this was a high risk strategy. Welsh had a long history of misbehaviour in restaurants (falling asleep in the soup, abusing other diners, rearranging the fixtures and fittings, balancing plates of curry on his head etc.), so I was relieved that for once the meal passed without incident.

We walked across the Tyne Bridge as twilight descended over Geordieland. Being totally unprepared with no sleeping bags, warm clothing, or tent, we realised that our careless attitude of "so what, it's summertime after all" had been rather misplaced. It seemed to get cold and dark surprisingly quickly, as we jumped on another bus. Luckily this one was filled with drunks who were dismantling the seats and breaking bottles with a commendable degree of enthusiasm, with the result that the conductress was too scared to come upstairs and collect the fares.

Bored with buses, we opted for some free rail travel for the next stage of the journey. This was very pleasant but we ran into a few complications at the destination where the Doncaster ticket collector, not unreasonably, wanted to know where our tickets were. He eventually summoned the police, by which time I was falling asleep on my feet and couldn't have cared less. Irvine psyched himself up and then went into bullshit overdrive, spewing out some outraged, long-winded epistle concerning missed connections, stolen luggage (with tickets) and wrong directions being issued by incompetent railway employees into the bargain – indeed British Rail were pretty much to blame for the whole debacle. He hinted at Strong Letters being written and sent to Prominent People in Government. The sergeant was just about falling asleep on his feet too by the conclusion of the tale. By this time it was about 1 a.m. and Irvine persuaded the ticket collector to let us through. Both men clearly wanted to go to their beds and they weren't the only ones.

However, Doncaster at the dead of night proved to be a stern test of character for two exhausted, hungry, near-penniless wretches with no roof over their heads. It got steadily colder. We had wandered around for ages looking for somewhere to crash out and eventually – being too tired to walk any further – bedded down on a strip of wasteground. The earth was covered in broken glass and dogshit, and was bordered on one side by the road and on the other by a huge chemical factory. The ammonia-like stench hung in clouds around us, permeating our clothes and causing our eyes and noses to stream foully. It was impossible to sleep. We lay there determinedly for about two hours growing colder and colder, as the fumes seized up our throats, causing us to cough violently. Unable to endure it any longer, we arose, with teeth chattering, to resume walking The Road To Nowhere.

As we shambled forlornly through a housing estate at 3.30 a.m., an astonishing sight met our eyes. Ambling down the street towards us was a fully grown, beautifully groomed white horse, which then strolled past us quite unconcernedly. It was a magnificent animal, clearly not a dairy horse or common workbeast. At first sight, I became seriously concerned about the welfare of my brain. The creatures were fine adorning whisky bottle labels but less welcome in deserted English housing schemes in the middle of the night. But at least we both saw the same apparition. When Welsh was undergoing alcohol-related aftershocks, he was more inclined to suffer visions of imaginary cougars, so in some ways it was reassuring that he saw the same thing. I kept telling myself that. We *both* saw it. But suppose we were *both* hallucinating, after breathing in some hideous brain-addling fumes from that fucking factory??

After grabbing a few hours kip in the bus station, we started hitching again. At this stage, I still hadn't managed to find out exactly what he was up in court for. He had that vague far-away look in his eye when I pressed for an explanation, which meant that he probably wasn't entirely sure himself. But it seemed that after hitchhiking north out of London with Hawk, they'd been lifted in a transport café. The Mancunian loon was sharing a flat with Irvine in the vibrant metropolis of Colchester – the latter had been so desperate to escape from his terrible Civil Service job that he'd inexplicably wound up at Essex University. Adventures with Carlsberg Special and whisky had preceded the trip, and Irvine had fallen across the steering wheel of a lorry which was giving them a lift, causing the driver extreme distress as he narrowly avoided plunging off the motorway into a field. After being ejected from the vehicle, they'd stumbled upon the roadside diner, by which time events had spiralled out of control.

"I think we were throwing plates of food around and kicking the tables about the place or something," he informed me, eyes screwed up in concentration as he struggled to recall the scene. "We might have been singing and shouting a bit as well . . . They put us in separate cells at the nick, as we were both making such a racket they couldn't shut us up. Well, at least not until a bastard of a *Scottish* cop was dug up from somewhere. He then proceeded to beat the shit out of me, which I had to kind of admire. In a way I felt proud to be Scottish, as all these wimpy local cops couldn't get us to behave, until this sadistic thug from Glasgow appeared out of the blue. By the time I'd finished counting my bruises I was beginning to actually *like* the man."

Eventually some brave motorist finally deposited us in Grantham – at that time just voted "The Most Boring Town in the British Isles" in a TV poll – and we stumbled up Blue Street, looking with longing at the pubs we really couldn't afford to patronise. The Blue Bull, The Blue Horse, The Blue Man and The Blue Ram. With such a colour scheme, was it any wonder that the blue-rinsed old boot who used to run the country hailed from here?

Having no idea of the whereabouts of the court building, we were forced to pay a visit to the local Constabulary to ask directions. Never a wise idea, in my view. This was confirmed when we entered the police station.

"*You* again!" observed the constable on desk duty in a broad Glaswegian accent. Welsh just dissolved into fits of hysterical laughter.

"Where's yer long-haired mate, then?" continued PC Simpson, referring to Hawk, who was also due to appear. "Well – never mind," he added, "if he doesnae show, this long-haired yin here'll dae instead!"

This rib-tickling display of Cop Humour had Welsh just about in stitches.

"Take him away now, Dave!" he cackled, pointing at me.

Not for the first time during that tortuous ordeal, I wished I was elsewhere.

After a short local geography lesson from the Weegie disciplinarian, we retired to The Blue Ram to spend what we could. Irvine developed a strange admiration for the pub's sign – which depicted a gigantic and scarily realistic-looking blue sheep – declaring it "the most aesthetically pleasing hostelry sign I've seen yet!" I thought it looked pretty silly myself and rather rudely said so. Perhaps Salvador Dali had passed through years ago after snorting chemical fumes in Doncaster and designed the thing on the spot. It undoubtedly held the attention though. Its eyes bored into us as we walked away backwards at closing time, its inanimate body creaking mournfully as it swung in the breeze.

We spent the night in a local park, where again sleep proved mightily elusive. As we lay freezing on a couple of benches, Welsh started babbling a load of shite about the Lincolnshire Axeman, believed to be responsible for the recent spate of unsolved killings in the area. Apparently, he had the disconcerting habit of falling upon his unsuspecting victims under the cover of darkness in exposed places, prior to horribly mutilating their inert bodies. I was so crazed with exhaustion, hunger and cold I almost believed him. Again, the plunging temperature finally spurred us to our feet and we walked around aimlessly until about 5 a.m., when we passed out on some other benches right in the town centre. The Blue Ram grinned down at us maliciously.

The early morning populace was not exactly overjoyed to find two Scottish dossers cluttering up the high street, and several spoke their minds loud and clear on the controversial topic. Why did the police allow this kind of thing? What exactly were they paying their taxes for? What, in a nutshell, was the world coming to? The latter two queries didn't overly concern me but the first one did. I didn't fancy a spot of early morning traditional Glaswegian cop justice. I shook Irvine awake roughly, causing him to roll off the seat, landing at someone's feet.

" 'ows it goin' lads?" enquired Hawk solicitously. "Enjoying the Great Outdoors I see?"

Not long after, as I sat there in the court's public gallery, I found myself in danger of repeating Welsh's performance at the police station. Fits of hysterical laughter were not far off. There was something so ridiculous about the so-called justice system when it went to such lengths to drag two drunken idiots halfway across the country to a building in a one horse (not to mention one ram) town, where I was the solitary spectator to a farce involving silly pompous old goats confronting helpless victims of drug and alcohol abuse. I looked on in alarm as Irvine produced a nasty flowery tie from somewhere and clumsily attempted to tie it around his manky neck. His face was equally grubby, punctured with bright red spots and offset with a greasy stubbly beard. His eyes stared out bleakly from his haggard face, completing the picture of wanton despair.

Hawk was marginally more presentable but his ragged arse-less jeans (which Police Constable D. Simpson had stated could have got him done for indecent exposure into the bargain) and long, flowing, unkempt hair also announced his guilt to the world.

The charges were read out. Apparently the Grantham Two had first broken the law by trying to hitch lifts on the motorway. None were forthcoming. So, in a fit of desperation, Hawk finally stood in the middle of the road to halt an oncoming car, which – luckily you might say – decided to stop. Irvine then climbed on its bonnet to prevent the driver changing his mind and shooting off. It was around then they noticed it had a funny blue light on the roof. So perhaps not so lucky after all.

BLUE RAM BLUES

The pair exchanged surprised glances. Obviously neither could remember the incident at all. But they wisely decided not to argue and pled guilty. Welsh went into his usual "naïve ex-pat Scotsman unused to strong liquor" routine, which has been trotted out in so many courtrooms up and down the land it's probably carved in tablets of stone somewhere. Still, it maybe sounded mildly convincing if you hadn't heard it before. His eloquence had alleviated many a dire situation over the years, but conversely had also led him (and more importantly his friends) into being right up shit creek with no fucking paddles in the first place. This time he escaped with a fine considerably less than Hawk's, but as the latter was the one found in possession of the Killer Weed, the result was probably much as they'd been expecting.

We adjourned to The Blue Man to discuss the merits of the English legal system.

"I thought you got pulled in a transport café?" I pointed out.

"So did I. You could have knocked me down with the proverbial feather when the old cunt came up with that version. Now that I think about it, I do vaguely remember clambering about on the polis car though."

After a few pints courtesy of Hawk, we bade him farewell and pondered our next move. Feeling fairly elated at the thought that we could now head for home, we descended on the railway station. After buying two platform tickets, we sneaked onto a northbound train and fell asleep immediately.

"End of the line! End of the line!"

I was jolted out of a dream, where the Blue Ram was pursuing me through the tranquil English countryside, by the repetition of this seemingly meaningless phrase. Where were we anyway?? I swung round to see the ticket collector walking down the train towards us. The situation clarified instantly. I urgently tugged at Welsh's arm.

11

"C'mon! Let's move!"

"End of the line!" repeated this helpful chappie, who was now only one carriage away and gaining fast. Everyone else had already got off and he was now checking the toilets. We scrambled out of our seats and tumbled out of the door, with Irvine still half asleep.

"End of the line!" he finally crowed in jubilation. "All the way back to Edinburgh for fuck all!"

It was then I saw something that caused me to leap about three feet in the air, before rubbing my eyes furiously and fearfully refocusing my gaze. No – it was still there. "It" was a huge British Rail station sign. And on it, in unmistakeably large letters, was printed one fateful four-letter word – "YORK". Many more four-letter words followed . . .

"YORK??" screamed Welsh in outraged tones. "What the fuck are we doing in York!? Fucking British Rail, screwed us around in Doncaster and now they're doing it again! York! We should be in fucking Edinburgh! End of the line my arse! I'm going to complain!" An interested crowd of spectators were starting to gather as I firmly vetoed this form of action.

"We don't have any travel tickets remember?" I whispered.

He paused in his tirade against BR and a thoughtful expression crossed his anguished face. "No, we don't, do we? C'mon then. Let's get to fuck out of here."

This proved easier said than done. There appeared to be no way off the platform, apart from through the barriers. The other passengers had lost interest in us but as we roamed desperately to and fro seeking an escape route, we were feeling more conspicuous by the minute. If we'd been a good deal fitter we might have jumped the gate and made a run for it, but the rigours of the whole ghastly ordeal had knocked the stuffing out of us in no uncertain terms. And even if we had summoned up the necessary resources, the station was really crowded and in our half-crazed paranoiac state, it also seemed to be swarming with BR Nazis and railway polis stormtroopers. There was no way through. I was on the point of collapsing in despair when Irvine grabbed my wrist and pointed wordlessly to a narrow metallic spiral staircase, which wound its way up onto the station roof.

Expecting at any moment to hear a shout behind us, we fearfully ascended the stair. But no one noticed as we climbed up and out at the top. The scent of freedom was in our nostrils. But not for long. I felt like a Lower East Side hood on the run from the FBI in some dodgy 1930s B-movie set in Manhattan. I could visualise us being pinpointed by the sweeping searchlights before a fat guard in a sweat-stained shirt picked us off through the sights of his telescopic rifle. We were clearly done for now, because there was no way to get *off* the roof. Even a good old-fashioned Scottish "dreep" was out of the question. Irvine beat his fist off his forehead in frustration.

"Where's the drainpipe?" he demanded. "There's always a drainpipe in movies like this!"

Well at least we were both in this film noir together. Irv poked his head cautiously over the side, like that of a recalcitrant tortoise emerging from its shell.

"No. We're fucked," he announced succinctly.

Miserably we returned to the top of the spiral stairs and started to descend. The only bright spot was the fact that despite being seemingly caught like rats in a trap, no one had apparently seen us or wished to question our behaviour. Not *yet*.

Back at ground level, I leaned back and closed my eyes. It was all too much. I could feel hysteria rising from within again. Then something behind me moved slightly and I struggled to regain my balance. I opened my eyes to see Irv staring behind me in disbelief. I had been leaning against a sliding door, which appeared to be some sort of entrance for Goods vehicles, therefore leading out into the street. Oh no, I thought. We must be imagining this – surely another joint hallucination? But as we tugged surreptitiously at the handles, it slid back slowly and we were apparently in the clear. Free! No one came running in pursuit. We cavorted merrily up the street, briefly flooded with relief and happiness.

But only very briefly. After all, not long ago we had stupidly anticipated being back in Edinburgh and here we were, still two hundred miles from home, completely penniless and hopelessly off the beaten track for hitching north. Life was still shite.

Some hours later, we found ourselves plodding mindlessly along a country road, thumbs at forty-five degrees. Another scorching day was slowly evolving into the cool of evening, which would in turn be superseded by the big chill of night. The sun was sinking down over the fields – a perfect scene of rural tranquillity unfolding, which was totally at odds with our mood. That wasn't improved when we finally did get a lift, as the driver was the sort of insufferably boring bastard who most likely spent his days traversing the highways seeking out hitchhikers to torment. His twin specialist subjects were Marti Caine and Scarborough Town Hall.

The latter was apparently about to "be..t..u..r..n..e..d..i..n..t..o.. b..l..u..d..y.S..K..A..T..E..B..O..A..R..D.a..r.. e..n..a!" His hackles rose in indignation at such an outrage. "B.l.u.i.d..y.T.o.w.n C..o..u..n..c..i..l..b..l..u.i.d..y..T..o..w..n..H..a..l.l."

Scarbore's incredibly drawn out mode of speech was roughly akin to listening to sharpened fingernails being drawn slowly down a blackboard – you wanted to clamp your hands over your ears and scream but you knew that the awful sound would continue anyway. "M..a.r..t..i..C..a..i..n..e..u..s..e..d..t..o.a..p..p.e..a..r.. t..h..e..r..e..a..l..l..t.. h..e..t..i..m..e.h..o..w..c..a..n..s..h..e.b.e.. e.x..p..e..c..t..e..d..t..o p..e..r..f..o..r..m.a..t.a..B..L..U..I..D..Y.. S..K..A..T..E..B..O.A..R..D.A..R.. E..N..A..?"

How indeed? I wondered idly about the merits of strangling Scarbore on the spot and burying his scrawny body in a ditch somewhere, before fleeing into the surrounding Yorkshire Dales.

Then again, neither of us could drive. Scarbore droned on interminably, blissfully unaware of his narrow reprieve.

After escaping on the outskirts of Pickering – which was even further off the beaten track than we'd been before being abducted by the Marti Caine Appreciation Society – we glumly bedded down in a graveyard. Irvine actually succeeded in dropping off for a while but inevitably the relentless cold gnawing at his bones soon put paid to that. All these nights of frozen misery were starting to blend into one Long Dark Night of the Soul as far as I was concerned. We had covered countless miles during the wee sma' oors by aimlessly walking, in futile attempts at keeping warm. But this was by far the coldest night yet.

We wandered round and round the utterly deserted village, casting longing glances at curtained windows on cosy little cottages, which probably had crackling log fires burning within. My reveries were interrupted as Irv let out something that was halfway between a muffled scream and a sob.

"I canny stand any more of this! I can't feel my feet any longer. I've developed fucking hypothermia! MARTI CAINE YOU BITCH, IT'S ALL YOUR FUCKING FAULT!!!" He collapsed in a shop doorway, gasping theatrically.

"What are we going to do then?"

His breaths slowed down gradually and the crazed gleam in his eyes abated for the time being. I could see he was considering the possibilities sensibly.

"We could try and get ourselves arrested," he said after a while.

"WHAT?!"

"Well, at least we would be out of this weather."

He had a point, I conceded. What a fucking choice, though – frostbite or jail.

However, we couldn't find any police station or any other place of authority where we could effectively create a disturbance that might hopefully result in arrest. And were we safely outwith

PC Simpson's jurisdiction? In any case, kicking up a rumpus in the ghost town of Pickering (which was so silent and bereft of life it was possible the entire village had been murdered in their beds) would have seemed almost sacrilegious somehow, or damned bad manners at the very least.

In the event, we walked five nightmare miles to the next village. A thick swirling mist descended on us round about dawn and we could barely see five yards ahead. Then the foggy shroud would briefly part and huge monstrous shapes seemed to float out of it before disappearing again. As it grew lighter, the strange effect was accentuated, with great sinister blobs hanging in the sky on either side of the road. Overcome with confusion and exhaustion, we lay down on the never-ending highway and moaned and groaned.

Some hours later, when the mist had lifted, we realised that the bad trip visuals were merely trees, rendered spooky and unrecognisable in the queer half-light of dawn. An old Polish guy was deftly conveying us down a series of frightful, precipitous Dales roads and my stomach was churning horribly. Every time another impossible hairpin bend appeared, I shut my eyes and waited resignedly for The End.

The lifts dried up that afternoon, as we shambled up through the awful industrial jungle of Teesside in the boiling sun. Mile after mile of greyness, smoke belching chimneys and machinery screaming – of all the miseries we had so far endured, this stage of the journey was the worst. The heat grew inexorably. My feet were so badly blistered I had to practically walk on tiptoe, mincing along the melting tarmac like a cat on a hot tin roof. Judging by some ribald comments hurled at us from behind a factory fence, I looked like a "tin roof" and all.

I tried to stride more manfully but it was no use. Welsh limped miserably up ahead, about thirty yards in front. When I heard him crying out to the heavens something about wishing Scarbore would tootle along pronto, I knew things were bad. And if anyone had stopped offering a lift for "one only", either of us would have gladly stabbed the other in the back for the privilege.

We walked right through Newcastle in the shimmering heat and out the other side, to a point five miles to the north. Then we flopped down by the roadside like rag dolls and waited for a lift – or death by heat-stroke. A never-ending stream of traffic screamed past us unceasingly. Seven hours later we were still there.

"Well – looks like it's just not our day!" I remarked in a desperate tone of mock cheerfulness.

Irvine shot me a look of loathing.

"Let's walk back into town and jump another train," he suggested.

"No fucking *way*. It's too far and we're bound to get huckled this time."

"I don't fucking care. Let's do it."

"No."

"Yes."

"Look . . ."

I stopped mid-sentence, as my eye caught sight of something most unusual. Irvine saw it too and blinked. Collective mind warp again? No. A car had definitely stopped.

The old bloke – a retired hitchhiker himself – drove us the short distance to Morpeth, which wasn't really much help. But it's amazing what even a short lift can do to revive the spirits. We felt a lot better as we resumed thumbing, despite being little better off. Within half an hour, it was growing dark and there had been little or no traffic. We were resigned to another night in the open.

So when the van pulled up out of nowhere and the driver shouted, "I'm going all the way to Aberdeen – any use to you?" I just gaped at it foolishly, opening and closing my mouth like a mentally retarded goldfish. Luckily Irv was quicker off the mark or we might still be there to this day. He gave such a hysteria-tinged yell of delight that our benefactor looked doubtful for a moment.

But we were in the back seat before he could change his mind.

"So what have you been doing down here, then?" he asked conversationally as we accelerated away. Of course we'd been asked this question numerous times over the piece. And up until that point we'd played it safe. Oh, we'd been at a party, we'd been visiting relations, we'd been looking for work . . . Irvine's story-telling skills had always convincingly fleshed out whatever tale seemed to suit the situation best and the motorist would be quite satisfied. Yes, I thought warmly of my old friend – get yourself in a dodgy situation and with a bit of luck, when smooth talk and tact is required, Irv will deliver the goods. The next moment, my admittedly exaggerated, rose-spectacled view of Welshy as a Muirhouse version of P.G. Wodehouse's Jeeves was rudely shattered when the reply came.

"I got arrested a few weeks ago and had to appear in court in Grantham," he explained.

Well, full marks for honesty, you stupid cunt.

I could see the driver's expression in the mirror. It was not encouraging. A large thought bubble had also magically appeared above his head. Imprinted upon it were two words, followed by a question mark: "AXE MURDERER?"

I tried to smile reassuringly but even if he'd noticed, I doubt the sight would have been encouraging. After all these days and nights on the road, I looked like a shattered, sunburned version of Charlie Manson on one of his off days. However, whether through fear or some other bizarre emotion, he drove us all the way back to Edinburgh anyway. I slept like a top for around twenty hours and awoke feeling fine, with scarcely a care in the world.

And then I remembered the Oxgangs Incident . . .

A LAD INSANE

Thin White Dukes of Hazard in Shellsuit City

The unintentional Jack Kerouac road-trip had mercifully come to an end. For now. We gazed agog at Martin Scorsese's sublime *The Last Waltz* up on the silver screen and nodded knowingly at Robbie Robertson's portentous words – "the Road has taken a lot of the great ones . . ."

Oh yeah. I was truly a battle-scarred veteran of the open highway now. I knew where Robbie was comin' from, man. The road hadn't taken me – but the Oxgangs polis sure as hell might instead.

I decided it was time to seek reassurance from my erstwhile travelling companion. He was a man of firm convictions after all – most of them for vagrancy, breach of the peace and drunk and disorderly. Although both fully paid up Rebels Without a Clue, my hatred of authority figures was more directed towards social security officials and other petty bureaucrats. I was fairly ambivalent about the boys in blue. My sidekick, on the other hand, was resolutely not a fan of the polis and seemed to go out of his way to provoke them at every opportunity.

"They'll throw the fucking book at you," he said gleefully. "The fact that you have no idea how you ended up covered in spew, cowering like a sick puppy in the shattered shell of a Lothian Regional Transport bus shelter won't look too clever in court, believe me. However, I've just the thing to take your mind off it. I'll see you up town at seven . . ."

I stood at the bar in The Grosvenor and looked around tetchily. Where the fuck was Welsh? He had made all this song and dance about going to a so-called "Bowie" night at the schemies' mecca known as Piper's and he should have been here ages ago.

"A Bowie night?" I'd said suspiciously. "What's the script with that then?"

"Just a night of Bowie music . . . and maybe some punters done up like the Thin White Duke," he'd replied airily.

I scanned the bar again and caught an unsavoury character's eye one more time. Shit! This simpering faggot was now smiling and waving at me, I realised, in a politically incorrect, homophobic flash of temper. Then a ghastly thought struck me. I looked again, harder. I moved a bit closer. Oh God, there was no doubt about it . . .

"What the fuck are you done up like that for? And what's with the shades?"

Welsh lowered the glasses daintily.

"Stops the eye-shadow smudging, darling."

I sprang back in alarm. He was wearing make-up, Spacey Tracey's scarf, a Miss Selfridge's jacket and a pair of PVC breeks. Ostentatious bracelets jangled from both wrists. OK, so we were supposedly going to Piper's. Piper's was in Lothian Road. Lothian Road at the weekend! Shellsuit Alley. Ned Boulevard. It wasn't that long since I'd narrowly avoided being stabbed there, having previously been mugged at almost exactly the same location.

"Irvine," I said firmly. "I am *not* walking up Lothian Road with you dressed like that."

"Why not, sweetheart?" He sounded most miffed.

"And stop talking like that!"

Ten minutes later, we walked up Lothian Road. I took care to keep at least ten yards behind him, ready to take evasive action the minute the first person punched him in the mouth. Miraculously, though, we arrived at Piper's with the Thin White Fruit still in one piece. However, my sense of relief was only temporary. We would still have to walk back *down* Lothian Road later on, when it would be even more dangerous.

Irv flounced across the floor to the strains of 'Suffragette City'. How appropriate, I thought, as I determinedly headed to the bar. In all likelihood 'Wham–bam, thank you ma'am' was still up ahead. I bought three pints, one for Irvine and two for myself, as two Ziggy Stardusts of uncertain gender sat down beside us. Irv smiled at me cheerfully, in an overly camp manner.

"Hi, I'm Jean," said one of them.

"I'm Jeanie," confided the other.

I took a huge swallow of over-priced piss water and tried to ignore everything. Trapped here in this alien landscape of plastic disco mirrorball hell. Life on Mars indeed. And what would these androgynous clones make of us? Just a couple of kooks, hung up on romancing . . .?

3

EVERYBODY KNOWS THIS IS NOWHERE

Future novelist attacked by black magic woman

Banshee screams in the dead of night

A barbed-wire place in the country

Twas the night after Bowie night. Talk about frying pans and fires . . .

"You wanna come up and see me some time? Like, *now* . . .??"
   Well, it was hardly vintage Mae West but the offer being put to us by Deep Throat was a mighty tempting one, even allowing for the slightly sinister undertones which accompanied everything that this woman said. We were sitting in a truly dreadful club, whose sole redeeming feature was that it stayed open until 3 a.m. at a time when everywhere else shut around midnight. The annual membership charge was 50p. Naturally the place was full of villains, cut-throats, junkies and whores: the latter two designations being within the remit of Deep Throat, who was now smiling at us in a manner she erroneously believed to be seductive. Then again, as she'd already bought the carry-out, I suppose it was to a degree.
   The company that trailed back to her flat in Upper Grove Place consisted of myself, Irvine, the Librarian, and some younger waifs and strays who we didn't really know too well. One of them was a junior member of one of Edinburgh's most notorious "fighting families", however, so we had reluctantly afforded the little shite some respect.
   Although Deep Throat worked as a part-time hooker, she was generally quite free with her favours when off-duty and

particularly so when zonked out of her tree. At this stage, her smack consumption was still at an embryonic level and she was, in fact, extremely attractive in an ethereal, off-the-wall kind of way, also possessing what one of the sexist young ratbags termed "great jugs". With previous close-up knowledge of these appendages, I was forced to concur.

As the party progressed to the strains of Pink Floyd's 'Shine On You Crazy Diamond' (a real hot dance number, that one), it looked like I might well end up on the dark side of the moon again. "Is that a can of Export in your pocket, or are you just pleased to see me?" slurred the hostess, dancing like a dervish in front of my prostrate body. God, the dialogue dahling, the dialogue. But there was a vague air of the faded, doomed thirties movie star about her, I thought hazily, removing the offending can and opening it. The next minute she was on top of me, accompanied by Orthanc and Zirak-Zigil.

I should have known better of course. Kooky people with varying degrees of drug dependency were distressingly prone to naming their pets after Tolkienesque figures, in my experience, but they had merely lost the plot. Whereas those who named their cats after *Lord of the Rings* place-names had misplaced the entire fucking cemetery, in my considered opinion. The woman was nuts, I decided. Probably heavily into witchcraft, too, judging by her extensive occult library and unsettling mystic runes painted on the walls. And there was something spooky about the way those felines silently followed her about. Still – great jugs.

However, the approximately sixteen pints that were slopping around inside me like rancid bilge water were starting to take effect. Orthanc shot me a particularly baleful and chillingly *human* look, as I felt the liquid tranquiliser propelling me to the land of shut-eye. In some ways, I was willing it on, realising whatever job Deep Throat might have in mind was well beyond my capabilities. I took the coward's way out and lapsed into unconsciousness.

EVERYBODY KNOWS THIS IS NOWHERE

Crashing out under such circumstances was always a bad idea. Terrible pranks were known to have been played on unfortunates who had nodded off at such events, ranging from their shoes being filled with soup to surgical eyebrow removal to trouser leg ignition. I snored on uneasily, jerking in and out of consciousness. At some point, I was sure I could hear somebody shrieking as if being subjected to sudden unexpected pain but it could just have been part of a nightmare. The shrieks didn't appear to emanate from myself at least, which was the main thing. In any case, banshee screams in the night were part and parcel of all our lives round about this time and were usually ignored. After all, if some selfish bastard had been fried to a crisp in their sleep, it wasn't going to do any good making a fuss about it at the time. It could wait until morning.

Once daylight broke through the grimy curtains, with a vicious disregard for sensitive heads, all appeared normal. Or as normal as could reasonably have been expected. The Librarian was still sitting there totally immobile, like some Easter Island statue taken root in the armchair. Awake or asleep, who could tell? As usual, he gave off the impression that he'd just been helplessly swept along by the Welshian whirlwind, which unexpectedly tore through his life on occasion. The latter had just emerged from under whatever stone he'd crawled beneath in the wee sma' 'oors. He looked even worse than usual, with huge great red-rimmed eyes staring out of his drooping face, like an ageing bloodhound that had been run over by a truck. Of the hostess and her Praetorian moggy guard there was no sign and the young team had apparently buggered off early doors. Irvine slugged listlessly from an abandoned tin of Export, retching immediately on finding it to contain a mixture of warm flat ale, cigarette butts and ash. It always happened to someone.

"All right, Irv?"

He just looked at me despairingly.

"Let's go to Glasgow."

29

"When?"

"Now."

"Why?"

"Why not for Christ's sake?"

As we sat on the stationary train at Haymarket, I could see that I was in the company of a man under severe stress and mental – maybe even physical – pain. Hence the irrational urge to flee to the west. I could sympathise to some extent, as the Librarian had filled me in on nocturnal happenings before we'd left the flat. As Irvine was doing his usual pregnant-mother-with-morning-sickness routine in the kitchen sink at the time, he was unaware that I was privy to the ghastly facts.

After I'd deliberately passed out, the sexually aroused Deep Throat had instantly checked her surroundings for a replacement victim. Unsure whether or not the Librarian was in the land of the living or not, she pounced like a sex-starved panther on Irvine, who was decidedly not. He was assuredly dead to the world, sprawled face down on the settee. But the hostess wasn't going to be denied for a second time. As the Librarian watched, she activated a switch, whereupon the sofa promptly shot out legs in all directions, instantly converting into a makeshift bed. She then went to work with a gritty determination, which had been fearful to watch. Removing her own clothes wilfully, she attempted at the same time to do likewise to the still comatose victim. Great jugs though, confirmed the steamed-up bespectacled voyeur. At that point he had also fallen asleep in self-defence. Or so he claimed.

As the train pulled away from Haymarket, Irvine was mumbling some sort of mantra to himself, which, with difficulty, I finally deciphered as combining both the scene of the sexual assault and the demands placed upon him there.

"Upper Grove Place, up her groove please, Upper Grove Place, up her groove PLEEEEASE!"

"Did you get down in the groove then or what?" I demanded impatiently, after several minutes of this.

Irv had his eyes screwed up and welded shut in a familiar display of deep inner pain. "It was hellish," he declared eventually. "I was so out for the count that at first I thought it was just the start of some weird wet dream. Then this sensation of being pulled and pushed around, and the settee or the bed or whatever the fuck it was jerking about the place like something out of *The Exorcist*. When I came to, I had no idea where I was or who the hell was molesting me. But she was *so* persistent that despite myself I started to get a bit worked up. I mean, she was topless by this time . . ."

"Great jugs," I interjected unnecessarily.

". . . Aye . . . Anyway, she had ripped the shirt off my back and I was just starting to get into it when . . ."

He stopped, as the flicker of pain creased his countenance once more.

"When what?" I prompted.

He sighed, and after a moment's deliberation, leant forward and raised his torn shirt from behind.

"When *this* happened!"

I whistled in admiration at the sight of the raking scratch marks running up, down and across his back.

"Jee-zus. She's a passionate woman once she gets going right enough."

He just stared at me with this haggard, hangdog expression again.

"It wasn't her," he enunciated through gritted teeth, in the manner of one goaded almost beyond endurance.

"Wasn't her? Surely the young team didn't attempt to gang-bang you as well?"

"No – IT WAS THAT PAIR OF BASTARDS ORTHANC AND ZIRAK-ZIGIL!" he yelled in agonised recall. "They must have thought I was attacking her or something, and both leapt on me at the same time. I just about shat myself. Just when I thought I'd got my act together, I felt this sudden searing pain in my back and all I could hear was this angry hissing in the dark. For all I knew that crazy, devil-worshipping bitch had set a nest of cobras on me! Orthanc and Zirak-Zigil! ORTHANC AND ZIRAK-FUCKIN'-ZIGIL FOR FUCK'S SAKE!" he repeated, slumping down in his seat, his life force apparently extinguished. Well, that explained the screams in the night, I thought, relieved. There was always a rational explanation, once you'd sifted through the evidence.

Just then, I became aware of the spaced out hippy chick who was sitting across the aisle. She looked like an anorexic version of Stevie Nicks and had a glittering-eyed Ancient Mariner aspect about her that made me instantly nervous. She was smiling to herself, as I inadvertently caught her eye. Taking that as a signal that cosmic communication had been established, she slid across into the seats opposite our own. Irvine was still slumped in his feline-induced coma.

"Have you ever thought," said our new acquaintance brightly, "that this is *now* . . . and we are *here*??"

Irvine opened one bloodshot eye cautiously. "Eh . . . well . . ."

"And if you join together 'now' and 'here' . . ."

"Ah . . ."

"Then where are we?"

Well, she had me beaten away. Irvine had come back to life slightly and was staring at her in much the same way that a stricken rabbit on the highway contemplates the approaching car's head-lights.

"We are nowhere!" she concluded dramatically, clapping her hands together. Irvine turned slightly, to stare at me instead. But this time his look clearly said, "Let's get off this fucking train at the first possible opportunity."

EVERYBODY KNOWS THIS IS NOWHERE

Alighting at the next stop, two nowhere men making nowhere plans for nobody stared at the ominous sign, and the high barbed-wire beyond. Carstairs. She was right, we *were* nowhere. But physically, now, as well as morally, spiritually and psychologically. This was not a reassuring thought . . .

A SPOT OF HARMLESS FUN

They think it's all over – it is now!

It was 1979 and the Decade of Bad Taste was shuddering to an unseemly halt. During this tumultuous period, there was always one option when things were getting too hot to handle in Festival City. This was, of course, to run away to London. Any excuse would do. Or none at all. We weren't naïve enough to still think that the fabled streets were paved with gold – at least not until you clocked the blinding metallic glow emanating from the mainly Scottish jakies' Carlsberg Special Brew cans carpeting the pavements of Euston and Victoria like an alkies' Axminster. But now the word was out for would-be escapees on the wrong side of Hadrian's Wall – Welshy was back living in The Smoke, albeit temporarily . . .

Irvine and I stood amongst the tartan-bedecked audience at King's Cross station and watched with interest as Benny energetically kicked a six-foot-tall skinhead wearing a Union Jack T-shirt up and down the platform. It was quite an entertaining sight. The shaven-headed idiot could not possibly have anticipated this, on foolishly approaching one of the most irritable men in Scotland to demand, "What are you lookin' at then Jock?"

In fact "Jock" had been looking for us, as we'd agreed to meet him off the train, but made the briefest of eye contacts with this now bruised and battered bonehead. Benny's temper was unpredictable at the best of times and it had not been improved as a result of eight hours incarceration on a vomit splattered Football Special. During the night, some fellow Tartan Army foot soldier had liberated a large Lion Rampant, a case of beer and about £70 from Benny and his sidekick Marsh's possessions as they'd slept, fatally pushing the man's tolerance level beyond breaking point.

As we decamped to Soho, it was obvious that this unforeseen calamity was now in danger of crippling our own finances. Budgeting for the Wembley weekend was difficult enough without having to subsidize two men with such prodigious appetites for alcohol, loose women and four-course meals. However, a stroke of luck befell us as we sat moodily outside a café waiting for the pubs to open. This was when a local pornographer offered us a stack of dough to help him clear a mountain of rubbish from premises he had just acquired.

We leapt to the task with alacrity. At some point, we were joined by two half-drunk Weegies who chipped in to lend a hand of their own accord. Whether or not they realised that they were undertaking voluntary work is debatable but it was made crystal clear to them come divvying-up time. As the Weegies were both about 5 feet 2, it was really no contest, as Marsh scraped the sky at 6 feet 5, Benny was 6 feet 3 in all directions, and with Irvine clocking in at 6 feet 1, I was very much the short-arse of the company. Wisely, the Glasgow punters refrained from arguing.

Buoyed up by this unexpected stroke of fortune, we took ourselves off to Trafalgar Square to splash around in the fountain for a while. I was the first to make a fool of myself, wading determinedly through the water as my fellow countrymen cheered me on. Heroically, I scrambled up to the top of the sole fountain as yet unconquered by tartan-clad adventurers, waving my own red and yellow flag in triumph. With that, a bottle flew through the air and smashed off a stanchion close by. It was followed by another and then another. Shielding my eyes from the sun, I squinted down to locate the culprit . . . yes, there was no doubt about it – Irvine was throwing bottles at me. Just then The Law arrived on the scene. I was too far away to hear the exchange that followed but it was dutifully reported to me later.

"Get in there and pick up that glass," ordered Plod, pointing to the water.

"I hardly came all the way down here to pick up English litter," retorted Irvine haughtily and was promptly huckled into the back of a waiting van.

At least it was now safe for me to make my descent. A tricky business and it was just as well I did not know then what I found out later, which was that a near neighbour in Edinburgh had been killed instantly at that same spot the previous evening, after drunkenly diving head first from the top. I rejoined Benny and Marsh and inquired as to just what the fuck Welsh had been playing at.

"You were meant to *catch* them," explained Marsh impatiently, as if stating the bleeding obvious. Benny glared at me accusingly, but then he glared at everybody accusingly. Quite obviously, it was my fault that Irvine had been lifted.

As I was the only member of our company to possess a match ticket, I left them grumbling to one another and headed off to Wembley. There, an uninspired performance saw Scotland go down 3-1, with only two moments of real excitement. One occurred as a bald bampot ran onto the park to attack an English player (it later turned out that he was English himself) and the second was when I suffered an asthma attack due to the crush. It was only by sheer good luck that there were no major tragedies in those pre-Heysel and Hillsborough disaster days, with the fans being treated like disposable trash.

After the match, there was more of the same as the police attempted to herd all the Scots away from the surrounding area and back towards central London. In fairness, this was long before the

Tartan Army had acquired the status of sweetness and saintliness they enjoy today. Then, they were regarded as a hideous drunken rabble and a menace to civilisation, and with some justification. Apart from Irvine, 449 of them managed to get arrested over the weekend for a variety of drink-fuelled misdemeanours. The muck-raking tabloids, which loudly condemned this behaviour north of the border, were of course the very same ones which attempted to whip up Bannockburn-Part-Two-type fervour beforehand. "Don't forget those bastards unfairly gubbed us at Flodden, now let's get our own back!" was the general tone.

Following the example set by many of the public transport overlords who had withdrawn their services, a large number of publicans followed suit and even in the city centre it was difficult to find anywhere open. The pubs that were open and willing to serve Scots into the bargain were the seediest dives imaginable. I had met up with Benny and Marsh again and we were busily imbibing in one such place when an entirely predictable fight erupted. It spread out into the street as combatants battled with pool cues, bar stools and whatever else came to hand. Scots vs The Rest. By the time the polis had swooped down en masse, one of our countrymen had been beaten and kicked half to death and the Old Bill corralled as many people as they could into the bar.

"We're looking at attempted murder," they informed us grimly. "Now, who saw what happened?"

"I did!" roared Benny. "There's one of the bastards over there!" as he pointed to some anonymous drunk, who was probably entirely innocent. Oh fuck, here we go, here we go . . . straight down the cop shop. They stupidly proceeded to put myself, Benny, Marsh *and* Benny's imagined culprit in the same car and the tightly squashed officers had a hell of a job trying to prevent further fisticuffs. One of the foulest-tempered men in Europe tried his best to administer summary justice on the spot but with little joy.

A SPOT OF HARMLESS FUN

When we arrived at the station, confusion reigned supreme. For a disturbing few moments, we were lumped together with a horde of guttered Glaswegians who'd been arrested and were in danger of being locked up for the night. By the time the mistake had been rectified and they'd got some rookie – who acted like he'd just joined the force that morning – to take statements, half the night had already gone. I inwardly cursed that idiot Benny for getting us involved in all this crap as the officer painstakingly took down my name and address.

"Edinburgh? Is that Edinburgh, *Scotland*??"

Oh Christ. No, it's Edinburgh, Papua New Guinea. This was going to be a l-o-n-g night all right . . .

"If we're going to be called as witnesses, will our travel expenses be taken care of?" Marsh wanted to know. "And will we be put up in a decent hotel? I'm fucked if I am coming all the way back down here to stay in some crappy b'n'b. I would expect a four-star job at the very least . . ."

By the time they released us, any public transport which had still been in operation had long since ceased. We wearily stumped off to spend the night in King's Cross Station. On reflection, it would have been better if they *had* locked us up. For despite amassing formidable experience in bedding down in railway stations the length and breadth of the land, I never could quite get the hang of it. It seemed that you were constantly under threat from a motley army of pickpockets, prostitutes, pimps and perverts, who tend to frequent such places in the twilight hours.

On this occasion, trying to sleep while the worst elements of the Tartan Army made the night hellish with their screams and noisy drunken belligerence was nigh on impossible. I did succeed in dropping off twice but was instantly woken up again by bizarre incidents occurring about ten yards away. The first involved some merry pranksters dressed in traditional regalia (Glengarry with four-foot long feathers, knee-length kilt, baseball boots and Lion

Rampant flag/cloak draped over too tight nylon Scotland top) who stole a wino's artificial leg and proceeded to play catch with it. The second incident unfolded as I awoke again, this time to the sound of running water. I opened my eyes to see an attractive, spaced-out black lassie with her skirt bunched up, blithely urinating on the concourse, and it was flowing in my direction . . .

In the morning, we decided to cheer ourselves up by taking in a popular pantomime, albeit one we had seen many times before. So we headed for the alternative theatre where Mr Welsh was featuring on the bill, along with 449 co-stars. The magistrate looked highly pissed off with this unwanted addition to his workload and clearly just wanted to get the whole thing over with as quickly as possible. He rattled through each "drunk and disorderly" with speedy efficiency.

"How do you plead?"

"Guilty."

"Anything to say?"

"No."

"Fined £10. Next."

And so on. Every misdemeanour apparently warranted a flat ten-quid penalty. All went smoothly until it came to Irvine's turn.

"How do you plead?"

"Guilty."

"Anything to say?"

Here we go, here we go again, I thought. Why did the silly man have to ask that? Irv spread his hands, with palms upturned, in a conciliatory gesture. He beamed at his accuser in a confident manner.

"It was just a spot of harmless fun your honour!"

The magistrate stiffened.

"What?"

"Just a . . ."

A SPOT OF HARMLESS FUN

"Yes, yes, I heard you Mr . . . ah . . . Welsh. So pelting passers-by with bottles and using foul and abusive language to police officers is your idea of harmless fun is it?"

"Not passers-by – *me*!" I felt like shouting, in suitably outraged tones.

"Well . . ."

"Fined £20. Next!"

Oh how we laughed, as did everyone else who had got away with half that amount.

But it turned out that the miscreant certainly had a more entertaining night than the rest of us. He had been banged up with about a dozen fellow Scots and was awakened only once during the night. Maliciously, after arresting a one-eared transvestite prostitute for administering a blow job to a client in Hyde Park, the police flung him into that very cell. The sickening noise of Glaswegian boots connecting loudly with delicate androgynous ribs was what had disturbed Irv's beauty sleep. The incident must have stayed with him, for he would go on to include it briefly in *The Acid House*.

We arrived back in Edinburgh penniless, the wages from our short-lived careers as pornographer's garbage-disposal operatives long gone (to this day, I still proudly list this occupation on my CV). And much to Marsh's annoyance, we were never summoned back down as witnesses to the attempted murder. Years later, he could still be heard bemoaning the fact that "A four or even *five*-star hotel, we were entitled to it, I tell you . . ."

HEARTS OF DARKNESS

Job-seeking in Jamboland

Shit! Bastard! That's all we need! And not even half-time yet! The
venue? Tynecastle Park. The competition? The East of Scotland
Shield final. The *what*? The East of Scotland Shield final. The
current score? Heart of Midlothian 2, Hibernian 0. The prognosis?
Not good.

We stood morosely in the decaying Gorgie Road end and
watched the scarf-twirling Jambos jeering in our direction. It was
not a pleasant experience. But what the hell, it was only a Mickey
Mouse competition after all (i.e. the final could only be reached by
defeating the might of either Berwick Rangers or Meadowbank
Thistle en route), it was hardly the league championship decider
between Edinburgh's two notoriously underachieving sides, was it?
I glanced at Irvine and saw that he was of a similar mind.

"Yeah. Let's fuck off," he suggested.

We left the stadium and turned right, in which direction it was
marginally safer to drink. Even having dispensed with the green
and white favours, it did not feel overly safe parading around the
enemy territory of Gorgie. After a short walk, we decided that The
Station Bar was as good a sanctuary as any. We got stuck into the
sauce eagerly, realising that it might be wiser to end up in a
moderately anaesthetised condition once the ninety minutes had
run their course.

At this time, once Hibs had gone behind by a couple of goals (to anyone), you could certainly write off any hopes of a comeback. They simply didn't have it in them. This was particularly true when up against their old adversaries, who were still smarting from the 7-0 thrashing handed out during the previous decade at their home ground, and were doubly determined to press home any advantage. The status of the competition was immaterial. We sat there imbibing stoically and gloomily, not really noticing the passage of time. For if we had, we might have thought it strange that with over an hour elapsing since our sharp exit, no other football supporters had yet entered the bar. Until . . .

"Shit! Bastard! That's all we need! And after extra fuckin' time and a'!" We looked up in surprise, to see an irate gentleman sporting a maroon scarf, fulminating against injustice as he thumped a fist on the bar. Before long, he was joined by several others of a similar disposition. It took a while for the cause of their distress to permeate our disbelieving brains, which had long since screened out any such possibility. Namely, that Hibs had clawed their way back into contention with two strikes in the second half, thus forcing a no-scoring period of extra time, and had then squeezed through 5-4 on penalties. One of Europe's – nay, the world's – most prestigious trophies was now back in green hands.

When Welsh had elicited this information from one of the maroon mourners, he just shook his head miserably and thumped a supportive fist on the table with a cry of, "Hibbie bastards." Of course, in a way, this was preferable (and a lot safer) than an understandably exuberant reaction but even I was taken aback briefly. It was common for him to adopt convincing alternative personas at the drop of a hat but masquerading as a Jambo was a new one to me.

"Been a Hearts supporter all my life. I came up all the way from London especially for this and just couldn't stand waiting till the end – when I realised those bastards were probably going to beat us – *again*," he was informing the maroon-clad confidant. The latter nodded in vague sympathy.

"The thing that really gets my goat as a *lifelong* Jambo," continued Irv, warming to his theme, "is having to admit that *they* have always had a better team . . . *and* a better support. That *really* sticks in my craw."

Oh no, I thought, he's overdone it.

"Now haud oan a minute there, pal . . ."

Don't mention 7-0, just don't mention 7-0 on New Year's Day . . .

"Hurts me to say it, don't get me wrong. Got to hand it to they Hibbie bastards though. Ever since they beat us 7-0 . . ."

Somehow we managed to extricate ourselves before his cover was blown. It was only a matter of time. To my knowledge, the former bogus fish farmer, Canadian ice-hockey star (retired) and personal security detail for David Bowie had always managed to carry off his deceptions, but operating under the influence of alcohol behind enemy lines was asking for trouble. We then strode back through Gorgie, loudly singing triumphal Hibs songs, which was tantamount to begging for a kicking, but reached Haymarket unscathed.

Now, impersonating a Hearts supporter was bad enough but I really thought he'd gone too far with his next Jambo orientated stunt. This was some time later, when the Tynecastle club were on the lookout for a new manager.

"I've applied for the Hearts job," he informed me over the phone.

"Yeah, right."

"No, really – I have. I just sent the application off today."

Tall tales, which would have been dismissed out of hand if uttered by a lesser bampot, could never be quite so easily pooh-poohed when Welsh was on form, I knew. Therefore, I calmly demanded an explanation.

CARSPOTTING

It emerged that he'd spent a great deal of time meticulously compiling a CV for the much sought after post, by conjuring up a past string of managerial soccer positions in obscure countries. He emphasised in his covering letter that he was, of course, a dyed-in-the-wool Hearts man, who had emigrated many years ago (thus justifying his employment with second division Cantonese no-hopers and up-and-coming Saharan outfits). To my horror, I actually realised he was quite confident of landing the job. He reckoned his apparent enthusiasm and global experience would triumph over the more orthodox applications, assuming that the Hearts directors didn't check out his credentials with Ogbomosho Athletic, Zhangzhou Star, or whatever.

Apparently they didn't. Or maybe they just had a better sense of humour than football club authorities are generally credited with. For he did eventually receive a polite reply from Tynecastle, saying basically, "Thanks but no thanks, and all the best in your future career." This gem, printed on headed notepaper bearing the Hearts crest, was promptly expensively framed and for many years enjoyed pride of place on the walls of his Leith flat.

Sometime later, we met up for a few drinks. One aspect of the whole affair had been troubling me and I just had to get it clarified.

"Irv," I ventured tentatively, "just tell me one thing. What the hell would you have done if they'd actually *given* you the job?"

"Changed their colours to green and white, then bankrupted them by signing loads of crap, over-the-hill rejects from Rangers, and watched them sink like a stone into the Third Division," he answered promptly. "What else?"

IT'S HER PARTY AND SHE'LL CRY IF SHE WANTS TO

Night of the long knives

Astro logical

Child abuse and shotguns

It was just your average Saturday night. We sat listlessly in the usual watering hole as a deafening heavy metal racket issued forth from the jukebox. In the corner, Puffin the Buddhist was talking to a dog and all around us, vicious psychotic bikers were doing drug deals, intimidating innocent bystanders and terrorising the bar staff.

I peered fearfully into the Stygian gloom. A Hell's Angel called Fingers (humourously named due to his distressing lack of several digits) was absently licking some crystallised substance off the blade of a huge sheath knife. At the bar, The Judge and Bananas were holding court, the latter's cowboy hat firmly in place. This was a worrying sign, at least as far as the ladies were concerned. His pet white rat occasionally came along for the ride, cunningly concealed beneath this battered leather titfer. At any moment, the hat would be whisked off in a lightning move and the hapless creature dropped down the front of some unsuspecting stoner chick's blouse. Piercing womanly squeals would rend the air with increasing frequency as the night wore on. There too was Barney the Beard, a huge biker from Bristol who'd somehow ended up on the Edinburgh scene, his mass of ginger face-fungus so extensive that he had got into the habit of tucking the end of it into his trouser belt.

Throw into the mix the spectral figure of Coffin (because he slept in one), Corpse (people never asked), Crash (who later burned to death in a mysterious fire) and a renegade American Hell's Angel called Preacher, and add in local worthies Tank, Stonewall, Stine, Rustler, Rampant Jack, Catfish, Plod, Hobbit, Santa, Pockets, Skull and Dr Death, and it becomes clear why Nicky Tam's of a weekend was perhaps not the best place to take your maiden aunt for tea and scones.

"It's too quiet in here," moaned Welsh morosely. "Fancy going to a party?"

I considered. "Where is it?"

"Wester Hailes."

"Whose is it?"

"Some woman I met at the bus stop," he responded vaguely.

I nodded resignedly. He was always meeting total strangers at bus stops and arranging future assignations.

"How do we get there?"

"We tap money off someone for a taxi fare."

I realised he was looking in Puffin's direction.

"There's no chance from that source. And if you go near him the dog will bite us before we try and put the bite on him." Irvine glanced again at Puffin corner and realised the truth of this. The dog was an unpredictable beast but particularly adept at launching itself, jaws agape, at human noses.

"Well, we must be able to tap *someone*!"

Ten minutes later, we were speeding towards Wester Hailes in a fast black along with the Girl With The Bird's Nest Hair. As she'd come up with the fare, we'd felt obliged to take her along, on the condition that she didn't talk about horoscopes. Against her wishes, we diverted briefly to Longstone to see if the Orange Liquid Monster was home. We reasoned that if we took him along as well, he might bring some booze, thereby saving us forking out for the stuff ourselves.

The Orange Liquid Monster had acquired his nickname in the best possible way – a chance one-off remark by Fox had seemingly set it in stone for all time. They'd been sharing a taxi and Fox had watched as his drunk companion slithered out of the door and crazily weaved his way across the road, his waist-length ginger hair streaming down his back. "It was like watching an orange liquid monster on the loose," Fox had said – and bingo! That was that. The man's appearance occasionally led to liberties being taken by pissed-up disco boys and the like, who would mistakenly assume that he was just some harmless hippy. But they never made the same mistake twice . . .

On this night, however, he wasn't in.

"He's gone to that pub he usually goes to," his deeply unnerving sister informed us tersely.

"Oh, the one he *usually* goes to," I said, as the withering sarcasm dripped from my tongue. "Well, that narrows it down to The Royal Mile Tavern, Nicky Tams, Deacon Brodie's, Clown's, The World's End, Archer's, Jenny Ha's, The Bishop's Remove, Jinglin' Geordie's, The Halfway House, McGuffie's, The Heb, Stewart's, Rutherford's, The Captain's, Sandy Bell's, Doolittle's, The Pres. Hall, Waterman's, The Candlemakers, The Beehive, The Fiddler's, The Burke and Hare or The Western."

"No," she said. "It's the other one."

We staggered back helplessly to the taxi and were met with a storm of protest from the Girl With The Bird's Nest Hair, as the fare had shot up alarmingly in our absence.

Still, the main object of the exercise was duly achieved. We arrived at the party and started drinking other people's carry-outs, which were hidden in all the usual places. Linda – the bus-stop belle who was holding the shindig – seemed to be a very nice if somewhat naïve hostess. The guests appeared to be drawn from the ranks of squaddies from the Colinton Barracks, bampots from Oxgangs and more bampots from the surrounding scheme. There was an ugly atmosphere developing even before I fell asleep behind the sofa.

Some time later, I was rudely awakened by someone screaming hysterically. It was our hostess, I realised, through the fog of stolen alcohol.

"I've been robbed!" she howled.

"Oh?"

"Well, *we've* been robbed!"

That got my attention a bit more sharpish. "Uh . . . how do you mean 'we' exactly?"

"Someone's stolen all the jackets and coats!"

Oh shite. I might not have had much money but what I did have was no doubt in the inside pocket of my retro purple, high-lapelled, charity shop, sixties fashion disaster.

"Brilliant!" whooped Welsh delightedly. "That fucking horrible jacket's been ripped off by some blind jakey. It's well worth getting my own nicked as long as I never have to clap eyes on that monstrosity again. Hear that doll?" he roared in the Girl With The Bird's Nest Hair's dainty ear.

"You're a typical Virgo," she told me sternly.

"But whit aboot the fucking jaikits?" demanded some other radge, glaring fiercely at everyone.

Next minute, someone entered the room to announce that the jackets had been found lying in a heap in the square outside, but minus their contents. The thief or thieves had probably pitched them out of the lavvy window after rifling through the pockets. A lot of confusion ensued as hordes of angry drunken people descended the stairs and started sorting through the pile. Accusations began to fly between the Wester Hailes and Oxgangs factions, and with the squaddies thrown in for good measure, it wasn't long before an almighty battle erupted. Residents from surrounding buildings gathered at their windows to either shout encouragement, threaten to phone the polis, or call out Neighbourhood Watch vigilantes.

I was feeling quite happy at getting my groovy jacket back and as

Welsh was also a professional coward when it came to violence (despite boasting an unparalleled track record for stirring it up), we returned to the flat. Linda was hysterical.

"It's ruined the night!" she sobbed.

"Not at all," Irvine reassured her kindly. "Up to that point, it had been one of the crappest, dullest so-called parties I'd ever been at. But that really livened things up!"

She renewed her bawling with increased vigour, while I helped myself to more of the combatants' cans. The Girl With The Bird's Nest Hair regarded us all with mute contempt. But I feared she was about to ask Linda what her star sign was at any moment.

Luckily, a diversion occurred at that point, which drove lesser considerations from our collective minds. Two of the amateur pugilists staggered through the door, one holding the other up. I glanced at the blood pouring from his stomach and realised that he'd been stabbed. There was a sort of strained silence, during which everyone wondered what to do or say. Irvine had his face screwed up in intense concentration.

"You can't beat Shalamar," he observed thoughtfully.

"*What*???"

"Shalamar," he reiterated impatiently. "Kings of disco music!"

"I'll phone an ambulance," said Linda, finally, in a strange robotic monotone. Now that the tears had subsided, she appeared to be in some sort of trance. The knife victim was clearly on the verge of passing out, as his mate carted him off to the bedroom.

"I wonder where his carry-out is?" mused Irvine.

It was not long before the ambulance arrived, with a polis posse in tow. In fact, a towering sergeant pushed his way in first, past Irvine, who had opened the door for him. It was possibly the last known Act of Kindness initiated by the bad boy of Scottish Literature towards the boys in blue.

"We got a report that someone had been stabbed," said Plod importantly.

"Yes – but do you like Shalamar?" countered Irvine.

"*What*???"

"I mean, are they to be rated up there with ABC and Boney M, or do you think that——."

I clasped my hand over his mouth tightly and smiled sweetly at the officer. He glared at us for a few moments, before stalking off, as Linda ushered him through to the bedroom. And it was not long before the victim of the blade also became a victim of the carry-out liberators.

Unsurprisingly, these events proved to have a sobering effect on the majority of party animals. People soon started to drift off, until we were about the only folk left. Linda made it crystal clear that we should bugger off as soon as possible, which we would have done but for one unforeseen problem. Although none of our horoscopes had predicted it, the Girl With The Bird's Nest Hair has locked herself in the toilet and was now having hysterics. We sighed deeply and started chatting up the only other two lassies left on the premises.

After an interminable period of begging, coaxing, pleading and threatening, our star-crossed companion finally agreed to enter into negotiations. Only after Irvine crashed through the door, seriously injuring his shoulder in the process, but eventually emerging with a wailing banshee in his grip. She became even more agitated as we insisted on taking the two lassies with us – along with a bottle of whisky – to a nearby garage forecourt. Although initially receptive to our pathetic advances, the fact that the Girl With The Bird's Nest Hair was battering us halfway senseless with her handbag and calling us 'smarmy bastards' at the top of her considerable voice had an adverse effect on the course of True Lust. Once the whisky was finished, they did a predictable runner, but not before we'd managed to tap enough for a taxi fare off them.

We deposited the Girl With The Bird's Nest Hair at the front door of her house, the make-up running down her face like a clown's, melting under the big-top spotlights. Irvine's enthusiastic rendition of several top disco classics from the Shalamar canon had failed to cheer her up. We taxied on to his ma's place, arriving there at roughly the same time as the milkman.

"Sshhh!" he urged, as we tiptoed into the living room. "Don't wake her up!"

I nodded soundlessly.

He then slapped Iggy and the Stooges' *Raw Power* album on the stereo and cranked it up to full volume.

"I'M A STREET-WALKIN' CHEETAH WITH A HEART FULL OF NAPALM!!!" bawled Iggy, as the Asheton Brothers' screaming guitars bounced off the walls and reverberated round the sleepy hamlet, probably waking up half of Corstorphine into the bargain.

". . . I'M THE RUNAWAY SON OF THE NUCLEAR A-BOMB!!!"

The noise was deafening, exacerbated by Irvine falling over a nest of tables while doing his air guitar routine, crashing to the floor with almighty force. He screamed in pain as his shoulder brutally bore the brunt again. The door swung violently back on its hinges and an enraged vision in a dressing gown and curlers stormed across the room, ripped the stereo plug right out of the wall, then exited in the same way.

"FUCK YOU, MOM!!!" shouted her son in a bad New York accent. He plugged it back in again and the terrible wall-shaking racket resumed. Shalamar might have been a safer bet under the circumstances, I felt.

When I awoke on the floor some hours later, I recoiled with hungover horror at memories of the previous night's events. And would breakfast be a strict no-no after the future Poet Laureate of the Chemical Generation's appalling behaviour towards his nearest and dearest? Amazingly, though, his ma came up with the goods, making no reference to the loud-voiced Mr Pop's disturbance of the suburban peace.

"And you'd better get yourself off to work," she informed her son.

He gaped at her like a startled fish, his face covered in blotches with red-rimmed puffy eyes. A three-day growth was rapidly accelerating into a four-day one. As the main man of The Stooges might have said had he been on the premises: "Your pretty face is going to hell."

"Work?"

"I thought you were working this afternoon. Double-time you said!"

His face was a mask of pure horror. "Work?" he whispered, looking in my direction desperately.

I smirked cruelly. At that time, he was working on the parks, in a manner later attributed to Renton in *Trainspotting*.

We left the house after an unhealthy fry-up and staggered up towards the 26 bus stop. Sunday services, of course. We stood there like arseholes for about half-an-hour until one came. Irvine refrained from speaking. His feelings were clearly too deep for words. He looked not unlike "the world's forgotten boy" as referred to loudly by Iggy some hours before, in that fine ditty 'Search and Destroy'.

As the bus rolled slowly through Corstorphine, into Roseburn and on to the West End, he came to a sudden but not unexpected conclusion. "I *can't* go to work in this state, no way," he announced. "I feel *horrendous*."

"And look it," I remarked encouragingly.

He turned his anguished face towards mine. "I think I'm starting to get the Horrors," he confided quietly. Well that was undoubtedly bad news. When suffering from the DTs, Welsh had a terrifying tendency to see three-inch high cougars running about all over the place. I was shit-scared that one of these days I was going to start seeing them too. It was obvious that desperate measures were now called for.

"That means we'll have to start drinking heavily," I pointed out.

A spark of life seemed to run through his diseased frame at this pronouncement.

"Yes . . . it does, doesn't it?"

We finally got off the bus at Portobello. Lurching down the road like two off-colour scarecrows, we entered the first boozer. It was a "piano stops playing the minute you walk in the door" sort of establishment but we were too destroyed to care. My hangover was raging with an intensity that indicated someone was drilling a hole through my head with a red–hot needle. Still – so far, so good. The cougars had not yet materialized.

We spent the next hour or so fully concentrating on achieving the Cure. Most of the regulars – who looked like they wouldn't have been out of place thieving money, jackets and coats while brawling outside Wester Hailes parties – soon lost interest in us and life started to seem not quite so bad after all.

"I wonder if the Girl With The Bird's Nest Hair got home safely," Irv said in mock concern.

"We *took* her home," I reminded him.

"Did we?"

"Yes, but she was still bawling and greeting and in a terrible state."

"Why?"

"I've no idea."

"Maybe we should give her a bell."

"Go on then."

He walked across to the phone and dialled the number. I watched puzzled, as after speaking briefly into the mouthpiece, he just stood there with the receiver glued to his ear, the colour draining from his face again. He motioned at me frantically, indicating that I should join him. I put down my pint and walked over. As I put the receiver to my ear he backed off and reclaimed his seat, grinning like a malevolent cougar.

"Hello . . .?"

". . . AND I'M WARNING YOU IF THAT GIRL COMES HOME IN A STATE LIKE THAT AGAIN I'LL GET THE POLICE ONTO THE PAIR OF YOU FOR CHILD ABUSE YOU BASTARD WHAT THE BLOODY HELL DO YOU THINK YOU'RE PLAYING AT FOR CHRIST'S SAKE SHE'S ONLY SIXTEEN YEARS OLD AND I'M SURE SHE'S ON DRUGS AS WELL AND IF SHE IS I'LL KNOW WHERE SHE GOT THEM FROM AND WHAT'S ALL THIS ABOUT THIEVES AND JACKETS AND PEOPLE BEING STABBED IN FACT I'VE GOT A GOOD MIND TO CALL THE POLICE RIGHT NOW IT'S ILLEGAL SOMEONE THAT AGE DRINKING FULL STOP LET ALONE GETTING INTO THAT STATE AND TO BE QUITE HONEST THE MINUTE I PUT THIS PHONE DOWN I'VE A MIND TO DIAL 999 RIGHT AWAY AND I'LL TELL YOU THIS IF HER FATHER GETS TO HEAR OF THIS HE'LL BE AFTER THE PAIR OF YOU WITH A FUCKING SHOTGUN . . ."

I just stood there paralysed. I didn't even have the presence of mind to put the phone down. Irvine was cackling uncontrollably and choking on his pint.

"Well?" he said eagerly when I finally tottered back to my seat, feeling extremely ill all over again.

"I don't think she likes Shalamar," I told him.

"No?"

"No."

"Oh – anything else?"

"Not really. Oh well – just a couple of minor points. She's probably phoning the polis right now with a view to busting us for child abuse but the good news is that her old man might shoot us first."

IT'S HER PARTY AND SHE'LL CRY IF SHE WANTS TO

"Oh. She wasn't too happy then?"

"She was about as happy as your average Jambo at 4.40 p.m. on the afternoon of 1 January 1973," I explained succinctly.★

"Jesus! That's bad!"

I agreed that it was.

The following week, we went to the pub as usual and watched Puffin talking to the nose-biting dog, and the psychotic bikers dealing drugs and frightening people. More than ever, the place resembled a subterranean bolthole for those of us who stubbornly refused to accept that the sixties dream was dead. The main bar looked like a 1969 refugee camp for acid-fried victims of Woodstock and Altamont combined. The Orange Liquid Monster oozed up out of the gloom and asked if we wanted to go to a party – in Oxgangs.

We declined politely.

★ Date of a particularly distressing Heart of Midlothian FC defeat (0-7 at home to city rivals Hibernian).

YOUR PRETTY FACE IS GOING TO HELL

Stooges on the road

Nurse! The screens!

Jimmy Shand

Going Dutch in The Clan

The mere mention of Oxgangs had unnerved me yet again, despite the passage of time since the bus shelter vomit sick puppy escapade. Were the cops cruelly toying with me? Biding their time before pouncing, to drag me kicking and screaming before a judge after a severe waterboarding in the dungeons of the Firhill Lubyanka?

"Yes, he signed this confession quite willingly, your Honour . . ."

This feeling of creeping paranoia was ridiculous, I told myself. That was all of three years ago, way back at the fag-end of the seventies. But as I involuntarily glanced at the 1982 calendar on the wall, the ill omens seemed to loom even larger.

It was the 13th day of the month. Not a Friday, mind you, but still the 13th. Saturday the 13th, in fact, as I glanced with some difficulty through the filthy window of my flat in Nicolson Street on the South Side of the city and saw Welsh striding up the road. He was wearing a horrible "bunnet" style Hibs cap, which had gone out of fashion about ten years previously. Not that they were ever really *in* fashion I suppose, except amongst hopeless cases who'd once thought that starry jerseys and twenty-four-inch-wide, half-mast Oxford bags were the height of sartorial elegance from Muirhouse to Milan. We were heading to Dundee and a cup-tie against United, but still had to decide on the mode of transport.

"Inglis says he's taking the car," announced Irvine, slumping into the solitary armchair and ripping open my last can of Export. "I'll give him a bell now."

But Carrick Knowe's premier lager lout and close neighbour of Heart of Midlothian legend Gary Mackay let the side down badly by informing us that he was going shopping with his wife instead. Aghast, we then tried to contact Sponge, whose moniker was derived from his formidable manner of soaking up the sauce – his booze habit had got markedly worse after his mane of tightly permed hair had caught fire in the West End Club one night. However, his assistance was ruled out on spousal grounds as well; in his case, the wife had slapped a rigorously imposed ban on the scar-faced fighting machine's attendance at soccer encounters for an indefinite period. Irvine had been present when he'd single-handedly attacked the entire Arbroath end at Gayfield in a drunken paranoid outburst one sunny afternoon – "I saw the maroon scarves and thought they were Hearts supporters," he later told the hanging judge at Forfar. So, with the chance of obtaining free travel rapidly diminishing, we decided to place our trust in that great British institution which had fucked us about so many times before – British Rail.

However, at Waverley Station, we drew another blank. The next service train would fail to get us there in time. We refused, on principle, to be pushed around like diseased cattle on a so-called "Football Special", which frequently failed to arrive on schedule either. The solution appeared to lie in getting ourselves down to the Easter Road area and attempting to gatecrash a Supporters' Club bus. We hastily adjourned to The Clan to make enquiries.

Four or five pints later, we found ourselves jam-packed onto the grossly overloaded Liberton Branch bus, having secured two seats at the front of the top deck. We had overlooked the alcohol ban and were sipping what remained of a half-bottle of Grouse some-where south of Perth, as I desperately tried to block out the noise emanating from my companion. He had been singing a medley of Hibs and Iggy Pop songs for some miles, and with "Your Pretty Face is Going to Hell" high on his hit-list, I was heartily sick of it. As the racket continued unabated, the bus started to accelerate as it moved into a long exposed bend in the road, which seemed to curve forever. It was blowing a ferocious gale too.

At first, nobody seemed aware of anything untoward but then the bus started to slew crazily from side to side, picking up speed at the same time. People started to shout angrily, thinking that the driver was irresponsibly having a laugh at his passengers' expense – perhaps he was a Jambo? But soon the anger had turned to fright as the realisation dawned that the two-storey vehicle was right out of control. Time seemed to slow down dreamily. Then the bus began to topple and we instinctively covered our eyes. There was a shattering explosion of splintering bursting glass and the screaming of tortured metal. We were vaguely aware of bodies tumbling around us. And then everything went suddenly eerily quiet and still.

Stumbling out of the wreckage, we looked disbelievingly at where the bus had torn up what newspapers would later confirm as being a sixty-yard stretch of the motorway's central crash barrier. Puddles of blood sloshed around everywhere. Before long, we found ourselves in the back seat of a stranger's car, with his daughter screaming hysterically – not surprisingly perhaps, as Irvine was bleeding all over her. Then, despite our dazed demands to "Take us to Tannadice!", he unsportingly drove us to the nearest hospital instead.

About twenty passengers were eventually to join us, most of them with amazingly superficial injuries. The pair of us were slightly more damaged, however, and the Bridge of Earn Hospital staff were finding Irvine a tricky customer. Blood-encrusted and concussed, he kept jerking around deliriously, trying to escape from a wheelchair. By the time they'd carted him off, I noticed that two of my fingers were hanging off, my head was bashed, dented and bleeding, my back was gashed, my jacket was lost, and a police sergeant was asking me confusing questions. I too was now wanting an answer to a question – namely, had my pretty face gone to hell? But a mirror reassured me that it was no worse than usual. Bad enough . . .

It was really only the following day that the magnitude of the crash began to sink in. Myself and the young Hibbie in the next bed gawped at the photograph on the front page of *The Sunday Post*, showing the aftermath. One look at what was left of the bus and we were wondering how anyone had walked out of there in one piece. There were no further complaints about our own minor wounds when we read that a teenage Hibs supporter had, in fact, been killed. Irvine and I could count ourselves incredibly lucky, especially as we'd been sitting at the front of the top deck, on the side the bus eventually fell on.

I asked the nurse who was combing all the broken glass and clotted blood out of my two-foot long hair where he was. She informed me that he'd been transferred to Perth Royal Infirmary, as they dealt with "more serious head cases".

"He's a serious head case all right," I told her. "But that's got nothing to do with the accident."

My own head was feeling none too clever either. After two hours of painful grooming, I was whisked off to have sixteen stitches put in it. They then dispatched me to an orthopaedic ward but after about an hour, I began to suspect that I'd been dumped in a psychiatric one instead.

My neighbour on one side was an ancient Jimmy Shand fan armed with a deadly cassette recorder, while the bed on the other side contained a guy with two broken legs who sniffily dismissed Edinburgh as "boring" when he ascertained where I was from – he was a Cowdenbeath man himself. There was also a football referee who was the kind of bastard simply *born* to his chosen profession, as he proceeded to order everyone else around, and a madman from Perth with a selection of ludicrously embroidered dressing-gowns – a Rangers supporter naturally. The ensemble was completed by a weird guy with staring eyes who said little but kept haranguing the nurses for my autograph. He was utterly convinced that I was Scott Gorham, the Thin Lizzy guitarist, and was worried that I might never play the guitar again. Well he was right – I never did.

It wasn't only the patients who were off the wall, though. An interesting routine was enacted every evening by the male nurse bearing the drugs trolley. The doors would swing open late on and the elderly patients would look up sleepily as he entered.

"PURPLE HEARTS! ACID! DOUBLE ZERO! SPEED!" he would cry suddenly, striding up the lengthy ward.

"Eh . . . naw, jist ma usual sleepin' pills, son," his charges would respond dreamily.

"Come on ya boring bunch, who's for the BLACK BOMBERS then . . .?"

He claimed to have been a successful songwriter in the sixties, even penning a ditty or two for The Tremeloes. "Bollocks," I thought dismissively, until the words of that old classic echoed through my mind – "Helule Helule la la la/ Helule, la la la/ Helule Helule la la la/ Helule, la la la." He was definitely the kind of guy who might have written that one.

"How you doing, Scott?" he inquired.

"I could do with a spot of whisky in the jar right now," I admitted.

"Still getting dizzy spells?"

"Aye. Thing is, every time I turn my head to the right, I throw up."

"You want my advice?"

I could see it coming but I played along with it anyway.

"Sure."

"Don't turn your head to the right."

"Cheers, Florence."

"You're welcome, Scott."

I was told I'd be in hospital for about a week, as my hand would have to be skin-grafted, but somewhere along the line, my sentence was doubled. Depressed, I phoned Irvine in Perth RI to indulge in some self-centred moaning. But he jumped in first.

"My pretty face is going to hell," he informed me pathetically.

"So what's new? How are things apart from that?"

"Terrible. The escape bid failed," he sighed.

"The *what*??"

"The escape. We almost made it, though."

"*Who* almost made it? What the fuck are you talking about?"

He then explained that himself and another head-case in his ward had fairly unrestricted movement, as neither of them had leg injuries. In fact, they were encouraged to be up and about as much as possible. So, at an opportune moment, he had persuaded his new acquaintance to join him "for a walk". Despite this dimwit's half-hearted protests, he had led him out through a convenient Fire Exit door and down the drive, where they succeeded in getting as far as the main gates.

"It was a bastard," he moaned pitifully. "They caught us just as I was about to open the gate. I could almost *taste* the first pint slipping down."

I stared wordlessly into the receiver for a moment and shook my head. If anyone else had related a similar story, I would have dismissed it out of hand, but where Irvine was concerned, I sadly knew that it was true.

"You'd never have got served anyway," I pointed out tersely. "Two people in pyjamas and slippers covered in hideous scabs and skingrafts walking into a pub – I mean, *pyjamas*, out there in *public* in the *middle of winter for Christ's sake!*" I yelled, as the full absurdity of the situation struck me.

"*Don't be ridiculous, we had our dressing-gowns on!*"

YOUR PRETTY FACE IS GOING TO HELL

"I thought your pretty face had gone to hell though?"

"My pretty face may have temporarily gone to hell but it's covered in bandages anyway. You cannot refuse someone a drink under such circumstances."

I sighed weakly and tottered off back to bed. "How's your friend?" inquired a nurse solicitously. "How's his *head*?" I just looked at her dumbly. What a question.

I was soon dispatched for some skin-grafting, too, and was informed on coming round from the anaesthetic that Hibs – having drawn the original game – had drawn the replay too. It ended 1-1, with Craig Paterson doing the business for the Hibees. And so it lurched towards a second replay. The Jimmy Shand fan's cassette was temporarily sabotaged and a radio was provided – at which point the rest of the ward suddenly unmasked themselves as rabid Dundee United fans. Even the crock from Cowdenbeath was pledging allegiance to the Tangerines. When Hibs went three down I stuck my head under the pillow and screamed for the drugs trolley.

Not long after that, I became convinced that Irvine had succeeded in escaping from Perth hospital. Four visitors dropped by, explaining they'd come via Perth, but there had been no trace of Welshy. They'd briefly considered asking someone but where Irv is concerned, it's often best not to ask questions. I had a vision of him absconding in a white coat, perhaps casually performing a couple of heart-bypasses on the way so as to cover his tracks. The possibilities were endless.

I was put out of my suspense the following day when he breezed in to see me in person. At first I thought the lingering effects of the anaesthetic were playing tricks with my mind. No – it really was him. He was already checking my locker for stray cans of Export and helping himself to Cowdenbeath's grapes.

"How did you get out so soon?" I grumbled.

"Ach, they just got sick of me I suppose."

I was then almost sick myself as he proudly yanked up his T-shirt to reveal the effects of the plastic surgery. His shoulder looked like it had been reconstructed out of yellow and purple jelly, which I lost little time in pointing out. He nodded enthusiastically.

"Every night jelly was on the menu I sat at the table bare-chested," he explained. "Everyone else turned pale and left, so I always got double helpings."

Thank God his face is still bandaged, I thought.

It was not long before I too received my discharge papers. Four days later, I was all grafted, stitched up and stapled together, eager for the off. At the last moment, the surgeon changed his mind and decided that if I was sensible, I would stay a bit longer. Well, I wasn't overburdened with sense and in any case, I too could almost taste that first pint slipping down. He was finally persuaded to release me, on the understanding that I would return the following week for the start of the long physiotherapy that was to follow.

Once back in Edinburgh, I felt more like undergoing psychotherapy. My girlfriend had ditched me, my job was on the line and – perhaps most amusing of all – I was homeless. My flatmates had craftily taken the opportunity to move elsewhere in my absence. I returned to where I thought I lived to find a bunch of boozed-up bearded bikers in residence, dismantling the furniture and throwing bits of it out into Nicolson Street.

Back at Bridge of Earn the following week, it appeared that my hand wasn't healing as well as expected, as I still had no movement or feeling in the two damaged fingers. It's a grim outlook when you're physically incapable of making obscene gestures should the need arise. The surgeon again wanted me to stay behind.

"What's the hurry? Why can't you stay here?" he asked.

I cast around for excuses.

"I'm homeless . . ." I offered, lamely.

"In that case," he triumphantly responded, "you'll be as well staying here as anywhere else!"

YOUR PRETTY FACE IS GOING TO HELL

But I didn't. I went back to Edinburgh and embarked on an intensive programme of groundbreaking physiotherapy, involving the concentrated lifting of glasses containing heavy fluid.

I was at this task one Saturday afternoon in The Clan when Irvine walked in, wearing that horrible Hibs cap again. I admit we made one hell of a pretty picture. He was still sporting a heavy bandage on the side of his face, covering his mangled ear, while I was still encased up to my elbow in plaster. It was at that point that a Celtic supporter with a face like a pit-bull terrier and a personality to match turned to his pal and said loudly, "SEE VINCENT VAN GOGH AND HIS MATE WI' WANKER'S CRAMP OWER THERE . . ." I diplomatically affected deafness. Welsh couldn't hear properly anyway but could tell he was being talked about.

"What's that dog-faced Weegie saying?"

"Says you resemble a famous artist," I responded truthfully.

"Oh yeah? Who?"

"Felly with a *lust for life*?"

"Iggy Pop?!"

"That's him. Now let's go to this fucking game. Yet *another* accident waiting to happen . . ."

GOLF LESSONS

Down and out in Duke Street

In sickness and in stealth

Seven years' bad luck

So Celtic had been and gone for another season, leaving a trail of broken Buckie bottles and discarded shamrock rosettes in their wake. Now it was time for a visit from the "Up Tae Wur Kneez" mob. Hello, hello?

> Oh I don't know why the Rangers say
> That they've always hated green
> For green's the finest colour
> That they have ever seen
> You can talk about your Alfie Conn
> And your Jimmy Miller too . . .

Singing lustily as we staggered down Duke Street – scene of Begbie's unprovoked assault on an innocent victim in *Trainspotting* – we were indeed approaching Mr James Miller's hostelry. Even in my state of intoxication, I realised that entering the establishment run by the former Rangers favourite would be a very bad idea, particularly in the company of a guttered Welsh. This was, after all, the solitary Leith hangout for those with a preference for the bluenoses. Even when legless, Rangers supporters were high on my personal list of "Things Which Made Me Nervous" – along with rattlesnakes, computers and aeroplanes – and I did my best to avoid them at all costs. With a nifty piece of footwork that would have done credit to Mr Miller in his prime, I steered Irv across to the other side of the road.

At the Easter Road end of Duke Street, we poured ourselves into what was then The Golf – a so-called "Welcome Inn". As we approached the bar, I began to realise that we were about to receive a welcome alright – similar to the one that the Pope might enjoy when crossing himself in front of the home support at Ibrox before a Rangers v Celtic game. In those days of frenziedly irresponsible binge drinking, there was one major difference between Irv and I when the session arrived at this crucial stage. Namely, that I could always appear sober enough to get served in a bar (although I might well collapse in a heap ten seconds later), whereas Irvine never could. That vital walk from door to bar under the stern gaze of the suspicious bar-keep had to be undertaken with military precision, but as Irv lurched forward with a gait like Oliver Reed on an ice-rink, I realised we were already on a sticky wicket.

"Two pints of heavy, mate."

"Naw. Youse've had enough."

"Two pints of heavy, mate," repeated Welsh brightly, as if the man hadn't spoken.

"I've telt ye once. Youse have had enough!"

"Two pints of heavy, mate."

I could see that Irvine's new found "mate" was about to become excitable.

"Get oot of ma pub – *now*!"

"Two pints of heavy, mate."

My companion's lopsided grin and ingratiating manner suggested someone who was trying manfully to convey a simple message to a flummoxed tourist who didn't speak the language too well. He appeared to be labouring under the delusion that if he repeated himself often enough, the nice-but-dim character might just catch his drift. Instead, the character in question came out from behind the bar with frightening speed, an expression of steely determination painted across his frightful countenance. A moment later, we were back out in Duke Street, feeling decidedly shaken and stirred.

However, one of the joys of boozing in the environs of Leith is that there are countless pubs to choose from. Some low dive would be bound to welcome us in with open arms, I thought optimistically, as we shambled down the street. This was merely a temporary setback. Irvine still seemed to be in a kind of daze but we entered the adjacent hostelry confidently enough.

"Two pints of heavy, mate." There was a silence of the pregnant variety.

"I said TWO PINTS OF HEAVY, mate!"

I realised that the silence extended to the other drinkers, as well as the peculiarly familiar-looking gorilla who was standing behind the counter, flexing his neck muscles in a rather alarming manner.

"Two pints of heavy, mate."

As he came round the bar like a greyhound out of a trap, I suddenly realised why. We were of course in exactly the *same* bar, having merely re-entered through the alternative door. Irvine had only got as far as "Two p——" when we were brutally bundled out into the cruel harsh daylight, with explicit threats of extreme violence if we darkened the dual doorsteps of the non-welcoming inn again.

One week later, we were sitting in The Burke and Hare, grooving to the sounds of Last Detail and trying unsuccessfully to unravel the events that followed our Golf outing. We had certainly ended up somewhere in Darkest Leith, but recollections were sketchy to say the least. All of a sudden, Welsh remembered he had an urgent appointment elsewhere and left the premises abruptly. And twenty seconds later, a broken-nosed bruiser who had gone to the Gents' reappeared and sat down on the stool he had just vacated. With sinking heart, I noticed that he was smiling ferociously in my direction and grinding his teeth in a manner guaranteed to reduce them to a very fine powder within a matter of minutes. He then picked up my half-full pint glass in his meaty paw and deliberately emptied its contents onto the carpet, all the while fixing me with this savage grin. I had a distinct feeling that he had something pressing to get off his chest.

"You and yer fuckin' mate were drinkin' in Leith last weekend, right!"

I thought briefly about denying it, toying even more briefly with the idea of imparting a jokey "pass!" in *Mastermind* mode . . . and then resignedly admitted it. He followed that up with an even more trying query, demanding to know if we were in a certain bar, which at least had the virtue of not being The Golf. But this was a genuine "pass" situation, as I had absolutely no idea, but again his tone left little doubt as to the correct answer.

"Aye . . . well, probably . . ." I ventured cautiously.

Perhaps I'd won the raffle or something . . .

"I KENT IT! I KENT IT THE MINUTE I CLAPPED EYES ON THE PAIR OF YOUSE! I FUCKIN' KENT IT WAS YOUSE!" he roared, banging my empty tumbler on the table in rage. Suddenly I gained a blinding insight into why that bastard Welsh had buggered off so sharpish.

It was difficult to find a bright side to the situation but at least the question and answer section of the quiz appeared to be at an end. However, the direct statement which then followed offered little respite. His knuckles whitened as he gripped my glass even tighter, his ugly mug contorted with fury. He had, I noticed irrelevantly, an extraordinary, tiny misshapen nose.

"THAT FUCKIN' MATE EH YOURS WUS SEEK ON THE FLAIR!"

Well, as original statements went, it was hardly a world-beater. Irv, I could have told him, had been seek on mair flairs than he'd had hot dinners. Cars, hotels, other people's shoes and my very own bath had also featured as receptacles for the Welsh vomit over the years. But this, I felt, would hardly console him. I still didn't see what he was getting so upset about, though, and I was frankly tiring of the rather one-sided conversation. The urge to tweak his incongruously sized hooter was also growing by the minute.

"So what?"

"So what? SO FUCKING WHAT? I'M ONLY THE FUCKIN' MUG THAT HUD TAE FUCKIN' CLEAN IT UP, THAT'S WHAT!"

Ah well, at least we've got that straightened out. Unlike your nose, I felt like adding but wisely refrained. His energy seemed to have dissipated with this final outburst, which had caused a silence of similarly proportioned pregnancy to the one the previous week in The Golf to descend on The Burke. He was then tentatively steered towards the door by a nervous barman, but not before warning me and Welsh never to venture north of The Boundary Bar again. It appeared that Leith was off limits for the time being.

There was one final postscript to our experience of Golf instruction. Seven years rolled by, during which time Irvine moved to London, played guitar with the Pubic Lice, went to Uni, worked for the GLC, got married, bought and sold property . . . while I sat in the Royal Mile Tavern twiddling my thumbs.

So all in all, some eighty-four months had elapsed since Jimmy Miller's narrow escape and Irv was back in town on a brief visit. He went out for a drink with his old Muirhouse sidekick Colin and unthinkingly dropped in at a bar in . . . Duke Street.

"Two pints of h——"

"NO WAY! NO FUCKIN' WAY! I REMEMBER YOU 'N' THAT LONGHAIRED CUNT!" yelled the irate barman, about to go in to his greyhound routine again, albeit at a slower pace.

"But . . . but . . ." stammered the visitor in confusion, struggling to ascertain the reason for the frosty reception. "But . . . that was seven years ago!"

"Doesnae matter!"

"You must be on some bonus from the brewery," remarked Welsh admiringly, as they were shown the door (and then the other one, just in case). The final Golf lesson was at an end and the 19th hole had run dry.

PEACHES

Walkin' on the beaches

The contrasts in the work/play aspects of my life were probably never more pronounced than around this time. I spent the days in deathly silence, buried alive in the Manuscripts Department of the National Library. Now, silence is obviously a good thing where libraries are concerned but this was really taking things to extremes. For a start, it wasn't even a public library, it served as a research facility only and as the only people I saw on a daily basis were my so-called colleagues, there was no real requirement for quietness at all.

The coterie of eminent professorial types who spent their lives minutely scrutinising ancient texts from a bygone age may well have been lovely people but as they seldom spoke to each other, let alone me, it was hard to tell. They were evidently from a bygone age too and some of them may well have actually been dead. They didn't even stir once a fortnight, when the Orange Liquid Monster would stagger through the Cowgate on giro day, howling drunken abuse at me from afar. I would hastily close the windows but the foul epithets were still audible, rising from the street fifty feet below.

It was a strange time. I hadn't wanted the job in the first place but the dole Nazis made it clear that no more benefits would be forthcoming unless I took it. The only light in the darkness was radiated by my absolutely lovely co-worker Sheila. On occasion, we would even exchange a guilty whisper or two. But overall, monastic silence was the norm.

So, compare that to a "normal" evening. That would be spent in the motley company of off-duty go-go dancers like Black Lesley, White Lesley, Queen Kim and Cathy Doll-Face, along with assorted flatmates, fat mates, musicians, dreamers, steamers, half-arsed poets, visionaries and petty criminals, in pubs where Hell's Angels juggling live rats was in no way considered out of the ordinary. Quite often The Haemorrhoids would be the house band on these occasions. Everyone strove for a rare vinyl copy of their debut album, *With Friends Like These Who Needs Enemas?* Songs like 'Pink Vibrator', 'Shithouse Blues', and 'Doggy Fashion' would always get the joint jumping. Sample lyric: "She got her kicks on the telephone/ Rubbing the receiver against her pubic bone . . ." Pure sexual filth and buckets of toilet "humour" were the order of the day here.

At the so-called "Pubic Triangle" of strip joints round the West Port, legendary go-go goddess Honey was packing the punters in. It was the first time anyone had heard of "silicon implants" – now you could see the "real" thing in the flesh, fake or not. We were on friendly terms with a few of the girls, as already mentioned, but Honey was *way* out of bounds, veritable royalty amongst professional booty-shakers. Then Black Lesley got a bit part in STV's popular soap opera *Garnock Way* and was feted from the stage of The Garrick to that in The Western and back again. Confounding all expectations, she landed the role of a stripper. She strutted down Bread Street in her high heels like an ebony-skinned Elizabeth Taylor, brightly beaded hair blowin' in the wind.

The Western also boasted the occasional star turn from a gentleman possibly named after Leonard Rossiter's *Rising Damp* comedy character. He was an old, super-intellectual vagrant resident in the Grove Street homeless hostel, who everyone always referred to very respectfully as "Mr Rigsby". After too many Carlsberg Specials he enjoyed clambering on stage between go-go turns and declaiming Shakespearian quotes to an enthralled audience of voyeurs and perverts.

"To be or not to be, old sports, that is the question . . ." his voice would boom, resonating down the length of the narrow bar. Rigsby called everyone "old sport" and was what used to be quaintly referred to as "a gentleman of the road". You never had to worry about lending him money, because he would always pay it back. He had a formidable knowledge of history, literature and world travel, and used to spin stories of riding elephants in the Burmese jungle at some distant point in the past.

Some years later a Community Project was launched with the intention of giving the homeless a voice, through a staged production depicting their everyday lives. *Glad* was so successful it attracted major media coverage and went on to enjoy an acclaimed run at the Edinburgh Festival. Needless to say, Mr Rigsby was one of its main stars.

When he eventually succumbed after countless years of rough living, *The Scotsman* afforded him a large obituary, completely dwarfing that of a captain of industry on the same page. Only then did we learn that one of the West Port's finest gentlemen and scholars was actually one Terence Francis Rigby . . .

Over the road, The Burke and Hare hit on the novel idea of sticking live musical acts on in between young ladies taking their clothes off to the strains of 'Le Freak' by Chic or Blondie's 'Heart of Glass'.

Then you had Charley, of Charley and Her Sheepdogs fame who successfully covered two bases. Go-go dancer one minute, rock 'n' roll frontwoman par excellence with her shaggy sidekicks the next. Charley was a pal too. Occasionally she'd request moral support from a few of us if she had a go-go gig in some unfamiliar place. Now the Sheepdogs' shepherdess was pretty damn hot but we'd seen her near naked so often we sometimes failed to recognize her when she put her clothes back on again.

On one occasion she was disrobing for some perspiring business-men in The Place while a group of us sat in the background discussing the price of fish or whatever and paying little heed to the show. The artiste was knackered, having a bad day in general, and had apparently forgotten that we were there for back up only.

"HOY! IF I GET MA FUCKIN' TITS OUT, WILL YOU HAIRY FUCKERS AT LEAST LOOK IN MA DIRECTION JUST *ONCE*??"

"Ah, put 'em away Charley, seen it all before," we muttered dismissively, as the familiar tattooed appendages hove into view. Cue for sweaty businessmen to turn pale, make their excuses and leave . . .

Pubic bones, pubic triangles, where would it all end . . .?

It was a lifestyle that seemed well-suited to The Pubic Lice. Ah, now there was a band. Or was there? Were they not, like Irvine's first group, The Southside Wasters, somewhat on the fictional side? It's a confusing business, rock 'n' roll, and never more so than when your aspiring rock star buys a bass guitar and eagerly takes it home, whereupon he attempts to plug it directly into the wall.

"Uh . . . you'll need an *amplifier* too, Irv," explained the workmate who'd sold it to him, once he'd scraped his jaw back up off the ground.

"A what?" demanded the Lemmy protégé irritably, dreams of instant stardom receding ever so slightly in the face of complicated technological terminology.

Welsh's first major bogus musical success was as my songwriting partner in The Southside Wasters, a fictitious rock band I fronted when living in that area. In other words, when we didn't have any money with which to go to the pub, we would sit in the flat composing spoof songs to the tunes of well-known rock classics. Among our best-loved compositions were 'Royal Mile Tavern's

Boring Farts Pub Band', 'Hibernian Rhapsody' and that ode to undrinkable beer, 'A Shiter Grade of Ale' ("We skipped the Leith Walk pubcrawl/ Upturned ashtrays across the floor . . ."). We even branched out into Tony Bennett crooner territory with 'I Left My Darts in Fat Sam's Disco'. For sure, 1983 was a year of dazzling musical creativity and experimentation. Occasionally, we would produce handbills for imaginary concerts and as we cheekily fleshed out the band with the names of a couple of real musicians on the Edinburgh scene, some of the more cerebrally-challenged rockers about town began to think the band was for real. We wrote literally hundreds of these songs, collated in two impressive looking volumes, which were later stolen – probably by Sick Boy.

So the dream was dead. But only temporarily. Soon Irvine had his amplifier, which went all the way up to "11", so just like Spinal Tap's Nigel Tuffnell, he could now play "1" louder. This would undoubtedly help his next venture, the punky Stairway 13, those mid-eighties mavericks who would go on to become the biggest ever band to emerge from Muirhouse, with the possible exception of Astonishing Confectionery. Irvine had long since vacated his old stomping ground in north Edinburgh but the rest of the band allegedly still resided there.

Stairway 13 were possibly an even worse band than The Southside Wasters, even if the latter never really existed. I realised this after Irvine lent me a bootleg recording, entitled 'Strictly Cowdenbeath' (this was a phrase he'd dreamt up, indicating that someone or somewhere was terminally un-hip or dull). It made The Damned sound like the Mahavishnu Orchestra. However, apart from the title track, I do recall that this proto-punk *meisterwerk* did contain one other genuine gem. Sadly, the full lyrics are long consigned to the rock 'n' roll dustbin but I still look back fondly on that poignant Welsh-penned love ballad, 'I'm No Saying Nowt Against Naebody'. The chorus went as follows . . .

CARSPOTTING

That girl from Pilton is a real sweet peach
She's goat mair crabs than Cramond beach
But I'm no
Sayin' nowt
Against naebody

Lennon and McCartney eat yer hearts oot. They don't write 'em like that anymore.

10

CRAPPY NEW YEAR

Captains' log

Yes, we have no Bananas

Tramp steamers in the bath

For bald acquaintance be forgot
He never bought a round
For bald acquaintance be forgot
He's lying on the ground
For Bald Lang Syme my dear, for Bald Lang S-y-m-e

Yes, The Southside Wasters were in full cry, befitting the special time of year. We were ringing in 1984 in the usual fashion. Someone opened a tin of cold Campbell's soup and emptied it carefully into the discarded shoes of the comatose gatecrasher. Jimmy Syme was a miserable old skinflint, a rail-thin hairless lanky streak of piss, who was also absurdly and freakishly tall, hence his unflattering nickname. Somehow he had inveigled his way into the shindig unannounced and was now about to pay a heavy price. He would almost certainly be set on fire later, when the bikers arrived. Then everything went black.

On awakening, the sickening pain in my neck and back of my head was alarmingly consistent with the symptoms resulting from being viciously dragged down a flight of stone steps. If this was a hangover, it was one with Bells on. Not to mention Grouse, Johnnie Walker and Glenmorangie. Suddenly, though, a brilliant oblong shard of daylight appeared in front of me and things became clear instantly. The reason for my discomfort was quite simple – I *was* being viciously dragged down a flight of stone steps. Inside a sleeping bag. Naked perhaps . . .?!

As I unwillingly emerged into the outside world, I ordered my courtiers to disengage immediately, while I furtively checked the interior. Thankfully, I was fully clothed. Fragmented memories struggled through my consciousness slowly, enabling me to identify my tormentors (who included Welsh, of course) as being guests at the previous night's Hogmanay party. That, I seemed to recall, had gone on until around 6 a.m.

"What time is it?" I demanded.

"Seven o'clock."

"Seven . . . you mean seven – *in the morning*?!"

"Uh-huh."

I laid back on the cold icy pavement like a diseased caterpillar afraid to emerge from its cocoon. Presumably it was New Year's Day, unless I'd been out cold for a full day and night. Why, though, was I being roughly manhandled about the deserted early morning streets of the Southside in my sleeping bag, I not unreasonably wanted to know?

As we entered The Captain's at 7.05 a.m., the joint was already jumping. The jungle drums had obviously been in operation, with the result that squads of alkies from the Grassmarket hostels were already busily getting tanked up. The jukebox blared forth, bass vibrations forming an unholy alliance with those already shaking my stomach. I peered through the pea-souper of cheap cigarette smoke, as a great cheer went up. Although I was resigned to seeing bizarre sights in pubs, the spectacle of Irvine doing his John Travolta act with some Asian lassie up and down the full length of the bar counter to some grim disco racket at 7.10 a.m. was even more way out than usual.

"Who's she anyway?" I demanded.

"Irv found her at a bus stop last night," I was promptly informed. That figured. The Lothario of Lothian Regional Transport stances had struck again.

CRAPPY NEW YEAR

Another round of applause went up as Irv and his partner took a modest bow. Two winos started to hopefully put the bite on me. The barman passed out. The door swung open and a scar-faced woman in a tatty afghan coat crawled in on her hands and knees. Perhaps it was time to move on . . .

As we wandered back up the Southside, Irvine irresponsibly launched a pint tumbler in a skybound trajectory. Just then, we saw Captain Cooper approaching. The Captain was the head honcho at the Sally Army HQ next to the flat, who unwittingly brought The Word to us every Sunday morning by means of conducting his brass band right beneath our window. No tidings of comfort and joy for hungover fools on the day of rest, therefore. But although we loudly cursed the Captain on a weekly basis, we generally got on quite amicably (at least up until the day we finally cracked, retaliating by means of blasting Motorhead's 'Ace of Spades' out through the open window via three-feet-high speakers).

"Morning lads! And, er, lassies!"

"Morning!"

Although I had one eye focused on the good Captain, my other was frantically scanning the heavens for Irvine's projectile.

"Happy New Year and God bless you all!"

"Eh . . . aye. Same to yourself!"

Then I saw it. The tumbler hurtled towards Earth like a miniature glass meteorite several yards behind the Captain . . . *but failed to break on impact*. An Act of God? It just had to be. (In homage, Irv and I later composed a Southside Wasters number to the tune of David Bowie's 'Space Oddity' but with the Salvation Army Svengali replacing Major Tom: "Ground Floor Flat to Captain Cooper/We are in a drug-crazed stupor . . .")

We resumed drinking in the flat, from the considerable stockpile of booze left over. Even the cheapskates we knew wouldn't have the brass neck to leave bearing whatever portion of their carry-out remained unconsumed, not at New Year anyway. The black bun, shortie and Tall Dark Strangers might have had their day, but at least this part of the auld Scots tradition endured. And who wants tall dark strangers gatecrashing anyway – more than likely they would be sporting black and white checked hats too . . .

I'd kept one beady eye on the window, to sporadically check on the situation directly across the road. But it was hard enough at the best of times to predict when Doolittle's might throw open its doors. Long ago closed down as a result of police pressure, this dive was populated mainly by radges from Craigmillar and the Inch (who tended to get off buses there, when "hitting town"), and members of the motorcycling fraternity known as the West Coast Angels. What the Angels were doing on the east coast was anyone's guess but tactical avoidance of the Glasgow polis was the most likely explanation. Indeed, the hirsute Vice President, Bananas, used to work behind the bar.

By the time it finally did open up, only Irvine and myself were fit for further carousing, everyone else having crashed out or wandered off. Although "fit" was a trifle wide of the mark, I realised, as I ordered up the pints. Irv had been teetering on the brink for a while, and suddenly it was as if an invisible assailant had dramatically whipped out his batteries. He passed out totally whilst standing up, in the time it takes to snap your fingers. Naturally, he didn't just have the decency to fold into a heap quietly. Instead, he slid diagonally right down the bar, taking all the glasses with him as he fell. The other drinkers stepped back smartly as Welsh ploughed through the air like a human scythe. Luckily for him, the big hairy bendy yelly felly was not on duty at the time but the stand-in barman coped admirably with the problem.

I watched admiringly as he dragged Irvine out into Nicolson Street and along to the benches on Nicolson Square where the winos congregated. He flung the limp body down, much to the annoyance of the resident Super Lager squad. At a loss as to what to do with myself, I left him with his head in some jakey's lap and stumbled back to the flat. I'd lost my keys and no one else was home, so I too went to sleep, on the landing.

On awakening several hours later, I retraced my steps back over the road and shook Welsh back to life. We wandered down the road to The Pivot. Here, Irvine impressed me mightily by succeeding in getting served. But as it was New Year, the bar staff were probably exercising a measure of extra tolerance, I thought. Not for long though. Delighted at his cleverness, he turned round bearing two foaming pints, smiling broadly. Then the old hand muscle paralysis set in with a vengeance. There was a loud familiar *crash* as the glass shattered on the floor, while I slithered off to the toilet. I wasn't going to be flung out of another bar for something I hadn't done. By the time I emerged, Irvine had thankfully disappeared and I quietly bought myself a pint. In fact, I was now longing for a concentrated spell of my own company. But there was to be no peace or tranquility just yet, as an old pensioner slipped and fell on the floor, cutting his hands on the broken glass. A momentary silence followed.

"It was that boy there!" barked an accusing voice loudly, as I looked up to see some muscular mutant pointing in my direction. Holy fuck, I thought, that bastard Welsh can drop you in the shit even after he's left the scene of the crime altogether! In a pub full of self-righteous drunk locals, there was little point in arguing. "Wasnae me – a big boy did it and ran away" would not wash under the circumstances. Grinning inanely and muttering apologies, I backed out into the bright January sunshine.

By the time I'd walked up the main drag, Irv had gone to sleep with the winos again. By this time they seemed to have got used to his presence, in much the same way as a pack of wild wolves will occasionally adopt some helpless orphaned cub into their pack to protect it from hostile predators. They snarled threateningly as I tried to shake him awake again. I was sorely tempted to leave him but manfully persisted until he reluctantly got to his feet. Some of the winos had perhaps been present at Irv's breakfast time dance academy in The Captain's and they were sorry to see him go.

We trailed up through the Meadows, bleak and uninviting in the chilly wintry sun. Hardly the summery nirvana of Sick Boy's squirrel-hunting exploits, as depicted in *Trainspotting*. Today, the great green expanse was utterly deserted as we wandered across Melville Drive towards Marchmont in the direction of Rocky's flat.

We found the tenant in a tetchy mood, as instead of being first-footed by a traditional Tall Dark Stranger, he'd had to settle for an Orange Liquid Monster instead. Not a pretty sight. His ghastly purple pullover mirrored almost exactly the lurid pallor of his face, indicating recent ingestion of amyl nitrate. The place was stinking of the stuff. In my opinion, this ridiculous drug was taken by rebellious radges purely because it *was* a drug, rather than because it afforded them any pleasure. However, it was also inexpensive and it was a proven fact that the Orange Liquid Monster would have snorted his own urine if the price was right. He was a veritable prince among cheapskates, I recalled fondly, as he glared up at us with undisguised contempt.

"The house is full of tramps!" he stated.

"Speak for yourself!" I retorted.

"Naw, I mean *real* tramps," he reiterated, waving a stripy purple arm vaguely in the direction of the bathroom. "Take a look."

It transpired that Rocky's eccentric-to-the-point-of-being-totally-off-his-trolley evangelical Christian flatmate had done his usual Season of Goodwill routine and rounded up some of the Grassmarket's finest for a spot of annual TLC. After installing the first batch mainly in the kitchen, he had apparently gone back out in search of the second shift. I opened the bathroom door and took an involuntary step back. It was the first time I'd seen a tramp take a bath close up, not a particularly memorable sight normally, I dare say, but this one still had most of his clothes on. He wasn't too happy at being gawped at, like some rare specimen on display in a zoo. He growled ominously, until he caught sight of Welsh.

"Awright pal?" he grinned.

It appeared that Irvine had well and truly been accepted into The Brethren.

Some hours later, as we sat in The Buccaneer, it became chillingly clear that a major medical phenomenon had occurred. Namely, that neither of us were capable of speaking English anymore. This fascinating fact was related to us some time later, by people who'd been sitting close by. They confirmed that we'd been babbling at each other in some strange slurred foreign tongue, possibly Serbo-Croat, which made perfect sense to ourselves, but none whatsoever to outsiders. This was a clear sign, though, that the New Year had just about run its course. The comedown would be slow and painful, and spread over several days in an attempt at minimising the withdrawal symptoms.

And then? Endless freezing cold days in dingy flats with inadequate heating. Darkness at 4 p.m. No jobs. Little money. Women? Seldom (and if so, generally deranged, on drugs, or both). Oh yes, indeed. January in Scotland! . . . is it possible to construct a more depressing fucking sentence within the parameters of the English language??

POSTSCRIPT

Rocky was not a man who enjoyed a great deal of luck with flatmates. Partly to escape from the Christian tramp saviour, he eventually moved to a new residence in South Clerk Street. Finding his bed there a tad uncomfortable, he got up during the night to check the cause of his insomnia . . . and discovered a loaded shotgun underneath the mattress.

After an even more sleepless night than usual, he chose to raise this rather awkward issue with his fellow tenants round the breakfast table. Both would go on to make the headlines – one locally and one nationally – on their subsequent violent deaths. Wee Alg, famous, amongst other things, for driving a high-powered motorcycle through the doors and into the crowded Nips o' Brandy pub one night, would later die after being run off a Highland road by a tourist. At his funeral, the motorcycling minister (with the wee man's body in the sidecar-cum-hearse) led a huge cortege of bikers through the city streets, stopping all the traffic between Leith and Warriston. Alg was an all-round good guy.

Sadly, his work buddy and fellow flatmate Jimmy proved to be anything but. He went on to use the shotgun to devastating effect, shooting dead a barman during a botched robbery at the St Vincent. He was quickly caught and received a life sentence. But it was not long before he succeeded in escaping from Saughton Prison in broad daylight and seemingly vanished into thin air. A year or so elapsed before the diminishing media coverage was suddenly rekindled, in the most spectacular fashion. We all sat agog in front of our TVs, as the *Six O'Clock News* reported the latest from the ongoing siege in central London. Police confirmed that the fugitive holed up in the parked van was escaped prisoner James Baigrie, known to be armed and dangerous. After a few day's tense stand-off, tear gas canisters were fired through the back windows, followed fairly swiftly by the sound of a single gunshot within. Jimmy had taken the one way out that ensured he would never be going back to jail.

Many years later, the incident was featured in a Danny Dyer TV documentary about one of the police marksmen involved in the siege.

CARSPOTTING

Wrecks on drugs and rock 'n' roll

So the cruel harsh winter of 1984 was assuredly upon us. It was every bit as depressing as we had fully expected it to be. Subsistence living from giro to giro on a strict regime of Pot Noodles and McEwan's Export, bolstered occasionally by free hot rolls courtesy of Speedy Maggie at Larry's Lunchette diner. There was nothing left to do but pull the duvet cover ever higher, snuggle down and keep the world at bay until the seasons changed.

Welsh lay face down on the floor for several days, occasionally babbling incoherently.

"Take it you've done the whole giro in a oner then?"

"Far from it," he croaked indignantly. "In any case, I've always held to the theory that the giro spends *you*, rather than vice versa. From that first seductive rustle as the postman teasingly slips it through the letterbox to the moment when it literally leads you by the nose, as you skip merrily down to the Post Office. You are helpless before the power exercised by that life-affirming sliver of beautiful green embossed paper. Soon, it will transport you to a world you never knew existed . . . or had at least forgotten all about over the last thirteen days. Then, the decadently luxurious sensation of the first pint slipping down your throat in The Captain's at precisely 9.05am, where . . ."

"Irv!!!"

". . . what?"

CARSPOTTING

"Shut the fuck up, eh?"

The minutes, hours, weeks and finally, months ticked slowly by . . .

In the late seventies and early eighties, the publicans responsible for Nicky Tams and The Royal Mile Tavern would be left crying into their beer at least twice a year, as the music festival season rolled around again. Edinburgh's two premier hippy/biker pubs would empty as a convoy of fume-belching cars, battered Transit vans and bikes would hit the highway south to Glastonbury, Reading, or wherever. But amazingly, this particular year, I had enough dough to finance a train fare to cover at least part of the journey. I then wondered if I would find anyone foolish enough to volunteer for the role of travelling companion.

"I'm no hippy!" Welsh would later bleat to the press when confronted by some allegations about his past, putting the boot into yours truly for good measure in his column in *Loaded* magazine. But it still didn't take much to talk him into accompanying me down to Wakefield. The fact that Jethro Tull were by far the most hip act on the bill will give you some idea of Irv's deplorable credibility rating at the time. In fact, I think Hawkwind might have been there too maaaan . . .

If you've digested the story "Blue Ram Blues", then you may recall how we once got trapped on the roof of York Station, in a bid to escape from BR officials who may have been pursuing us for travelling with no tickets. So, it was with some trepidation that we alighted at the very destination, half expecting to see "WANTED – DEAD OR ALIVE" type posters bearing our mug shots tacked up everywhere. In any case, Welsh has had a long and dishonourable record of misbehaving outrageously in railway stations for some reason, even kicking off 1999 with a celebrity arrest in Exeter St Davids. (When I saw the screaming newspaper headline "SCOTTISH AUTHOR ARRESTED IN EXETER!"

CARSPOTTING

I didn't exactly have to wrack my brain to hazard a guess as to his identity. Put it this way, I never thought it was going to be Alexander McCall Smith.)

But that ridiculous charade was still fifteen years away. Presently, we were already quite drunk and not particularly looking forward to hitching the rest of the way, when someone yelled at us from a passing car window. We blanched fearfully. It's never a good sign getting recognised by the populace in strange towns, especially if you've got a guilty conscience over previous crimes committed in the area. But it turned out to be our old acquaintance Skinny, who was also heading for the festival, which was a good thing. The bad thing was he was travelling with the Strychnine Sisters.

The previous year, the fearsome females had consented to giving myself, Catfish, Skinny and Luscious Linda a lift to Glastonbury. Somewhere on the M6, the driver had complained of tiredness and Skinny had kindly offered to take the wheel for a while.

"Are you sure you're fit to drive?"

"Oh, aye," he'd said reassuringly, between glugs of whisky.

Ten minutes later, there was a hideous screeching sound as we sheared into another vehicle going in the same direction at 80 m.p.h. Our car spun dizzyingly across the central reservation, eventually coming to a halt facing back the way we had come. If there hadn't been a fortuitous break in the barriers or if any traffic had been heading north, we'd almost certainly have all been killed or, at the very least, horribly mangled.

The Glaswegian family whose holiday (and car) Skinny had just successfully ruined were busy freaking out by the roadside. But mercifully, they seemed fairly unscathed, apart from clearly suffering from shock. Unfortunately, though, they weren't shocked enough to overlook summoning the polis from one of the emergency phones.

As the boys in blue pulled up, Strychnine Sister No. 1 posed a rather pertinent but downright foolish question. "Are there any drugs in the car?"

There was a momentary silence.

"I've got a lump of black . . . and some speed too," admitted Skinny.

"There's acid in the glove compartment," I reminded her helpfully.

There wasn't even any point in asking Luscious – she was so out of it on downers that she wasn't even aware that we'd crashed. As one of the cops slowly started walking towards us, we all turned and looked nervously at Catfish.

"So that's hash, speed, acid and a shitload of Valium for a start," I said. "Any advance on that?"

There was another short silence.

". . . I think I've got a bag of smack in my jacket, man," said Catfish vaguely, just as the policeman stopped to talk to Strychnine Sister No. 2. She'd very sensibly got out of the car to try and forestall them.

The other cop was peering in suspiciously and examining us by torchlight. Two grimy, long-haired bikers wearing filthy cut-downs and originals, a dodgy hippy type in an embroidered denim jacket and headband, and a stupefied crazy woman who was slowly coming round and starting to howl like a demented dog. Not for the first time in my life, I was absolutely certain that *this* time I was *definitely* heading for the slammer.

Ultimately, we only got away with it because Strychnine Sister No. 2 took the brave but highly risky step of claiming that she'd been behind the wheel when we crashed. Luckily, the Glaswegians were in no position to contradict this, as we'd hit them from the rear so they hadn't got the full picture and were still in shock anyway. Maybe the cops just couldn't be bothered by all this unwanted late night aggravation. They ordered us out of the car and questioned us in a desultory fashion, but in the long run seemed content to accept this explanation. Just as well – Skinny probably didn't even have a license and would have been about four times over the legal limit, *minimum*.

It has to be borne in mind that we were incredibly lucky to get away with such leniency, as the mid eighties were an extremely stressful time in Britain (but particularly in Southern England) for anyone who looked a bit "different". The inner cities were exploding in major riots after years of simmering resentment towards Thatcherite policies, and the escalating miners' strike and attendant pitched battles between pickets and police were getting uglier by the day.

Even though we might have deserved the police's attention on this occasion, many friends were subjected to worse scrutiny, seemingly for no reason at all. Anyone in the least bit "alternative" was fair game for the authorities now. Longhairs were routinely harassed, lifted and questioned, despite having done nothing wrong. Friends of mine who were also travelling to Glastonbury were unceremoniously jerked off a train two hundred miles north of their destination and taken to the nearest police station, where they were questioned and strip-searched. Sandra was six months pregnant at the time. Why did this happen? Their appearance marked them out as "hippies", probably intent on reaching Stonehenge, which was increasingly the focus of Government determination to clamp down on "The Alternative Society". Not since the embryonic years of 1960s counter-culture had such an attack been mounted on "undesirables". Sleaze-bag, fat-cat Tory politicians stood up in Parliament and denounced hippies and travellers in language that would have seen them dragged before the Race Relations Board had it been applied to Blacks or Jews. "Medieval brigands" and "criminal scum" were two of the less offensive descriptions. Well, fuck them, if that's what they thought of us, may as well take it all the way – was the general consensus.

It was Them and Us now, no doubt about it. This festering

antipathy would culminate in the horrifying spectacle of "The Battle of the Beanfield" in 1985, when hundreds of police thugs viciously attacked and beat up travellers (women included) trying to reach Stonehenge to celebrate the Summer Solstice. It was a nasty, brutish time in which to be alive in England's green and not-so-pleasant land.

But right at this moment, it was an understandably not-so-pleasant welcome from the Strychnine girls. I was guilty by association from the previous year's near calamity. As for Irvine – well, they just knew he could be bad news anyway.

It was always a mystery why the sisters bothered going to outdoor rock festivals in the first place. On day one, they would be complaining about the weather, the fact that they had to sleep in a tent and that the toilet facilities left a lot to be desired. On day two, they would be complaining that they had nowhere to apply their make-up properly, no hygienic spot in which to brush their teeth and that there was a lack of showering availability. On day three, they would be at each other's throats and those of everybody in close proximity. Then they would storm off in a huff, declaring, "Never again!" while we would yell, "Never say never again!" because they'd be back again the following year, complaining about the mud and the fact that Stonehenge was just too stony.

Nevertheless, we jumped gleefully into the back seat and helped ourselves to Skinny's whisky. The driver and co-driver greeted us with a frosty politeness that spoke volumes. After hiring a car, they had set out with plenty time to spare, intending to spend a couple of days in some picturesque spot en route. Instead, they'd been obliged to pick up Skinny, who was hitching south of Biggar, and had then led them on a wild goose chase all around his favourite pubs in the Borders region. They were Not Happy. They hadn't wanted to pick us up either, we learned later, but after the Thin One gave us the shout, they couldn't very well refuse. Irvine and whisky were a bad mix at the best of times. I could see them eyeing us nervously in the mirror and I hoped that he wouldn't start singing Shalamar songs. At least, not just yet . . .

We stopped off at one of those terrible soulless barns of countrified gentility which pass for bars in Merrie England – the sort where mine host has mutton-chop whiskers like Amos Brearley who used to be in *Emmerdale Farm*, peopled by upper-class twits with their 2.8 precocious brats, country toffs in green wellies and wildlife-slaughtering country "sports" bastards, not to mention rich landowners who absolutely hate their sanctuaries being invaded by weird, wild-looking, long-haired, drunken, scruffy Scottish idiots but are generally too frightened to refuse you to your face. However, by the time Irvine had dropped his fourth pint glass with a resounding *SMASH* on the stone floor, I realised that the first red card of the weekend might be on its way. His genius for dropping pint tumblers on pub floors was one I'd long admired but never succeeded in emulating. The trick appeared to lie in taking hold of the pint glass when handed to him but so slightly that the fingers did not really grip at all. Therefore it fits in the space between the thumb and the other digits lightly, instantly sliding out once the fingers are even marginally relaxed.

But this time it was another similar trick of his that finally got Amos to give us the boot. He'd tolerated the broken glass, the Shalamar records on the jukebox, the beer spilled over the pool table, illegal jazz cigarettes being lit up and Hibs songs being performed, but when Welsh started dropping the pool cue over and over *and over* again on the floor with a sickening, infuriating, nerve-shredding *crash*, he finally flipped. The Strychnine Sisters turned crimson with shame as we were propelled gently but firmly toward the door.

"YOU CAN'T DO THIS TO US!" Irvine yelled. "I KNOW THE CHIEF CONSTABLE!" We drove away in silence but were greatly cheered by the spectacle up ahead. The air was filled with the thunderous roar of motorcycle engines, and we watched in immense satisfaction as a huge phalanx of fearsome looking dudes and desperados astride Harleys swept past us and pulled up abruptly at the sign of the boozer. Tough luck if they fancied a game of pool though. Most of the cues were artistically splintered from tip to bottom.

We arrived at the festival site just as dusk was falling. Piling out of the car, we wondered what to do next. Skinny's whisky was finished and he was also adopting a rather frosty attitude towards his dear friends. Irvine was, as usual, mainly to blame for this state of affairs. The tranquil peace of the Yorkshire twilight was then broken by the strident voice of authority, i.e. Strychnine Sister No. 1.

"Where are you going to pitch your tent?" she asked pointedly.

"What tent?"

"What . . . you mean you don't have a *tent*? *None* of you??"

I looked at Irvine. Irvine looked at Skinny. Skinny looked at his feet.

"Well . . . really!"

"You certainly can't share *our* tent," chipped in Strychnine Sister No. 2.

"That's OK."

"We'll just sleep in the car," declared Irvine.

"Oh you will, will you?"

Irvine looked at me. I looked at Skinny. Skinny cleared his throat and muttered something, which might have been, "Well why not?"

"We'll not make a mess of it," I put in reassuringly.

The sisters proceeded to live up to their name by bestowing poisonous looks on the three tentless fools before them.

"That's a *hired* car, remember. It's *not* ours. It cost a *lot* to hire – and a *large* deposit against any damage."

"Message understood."

So we slept in the car. The first morning, the interior mess wasn't too bad. A few mysterious stains, some cold chips, empty beer cans and roaches, but no obvious burns in the upholstery or anything like that. We stood to attention as the Poison Girls came to suspiciously check for any signs of wear and tear. While they were doing this, they complained about the weather, the fact that they'd had to sleep in a tent and that the toilet facilities left a lot to be desired.

We set off to hunt down the rest of the Edinburgh team and found the Orange Liquid Monster in the medical tent. He'd badly sprained his ankle after climbing over the fence under cover of darkness to avoid paying.

"Go and buy us a carry-oot," he demanded in his usual abrasive fashion.

"Give us the money then."

"You shouldn't drink on an empty stomach," asserted a medic, rather fruitlessly.

After reluctantly parting with the dough, he gave us instructions as to his requirements (a dozen cans of the cheapest lager possible and a bottle of vodka). The Orange Liquid Monster was a fantastic cheapskate where carry-outs were concerned, forever extolling the delights of the most undrinkable supermarket piss-water imaginable . . . as long as it was dirt-cheap. He considered buying twelve cans of insipid yellow fluid as opposed to six cans of something decent an unmissable bargain, despite the fact that the latter might be three times the strength of the former. He hirpled along as far as the perimeter fence to watch us go.

". . . and hurry the fuck up!"

"Half an hour tops!" Irvine shouted back reassuringly.

Three hours later, we were still sitting in the beer garden at The Spread Eagle, socialising heartily with a most unusual policeman. He had taken a liking to one of our associates' "Don't Walk on the Grass – Smoke It" badge, which sported a large cannabis leaf.

"I collect badges – but I've not seen *that* one before," he said admiringly.

"You want it?" said Rocky.

"Eh . . . oh yeah, thanks . . . that's very good of you."

He pinned it on his tie proudly. "That'll shake 'em up back at the station!"

We agreed that it probably would. I then took a photo of him pointing at the offending article, wondering idly what the reaction of the tabloids would be if a blown-up copy was anonymously posted to them.

CRAZY CANNABIS COP CALLS FOR WIDESPREAD MARIJUANA ABUSE!

POT-MAD POLICE IN JOINT OPERATION!

LAIDBACK LAW SAYS "HAVE A BLAW"!

We drifted back to the site in the afternoon, absent-mindedly drinking the Orange Liquid Monster's carry-out as we went. He would be in a filthy mood but as that was his usual demeanour anyway, we were quite used to it. He would probably become violent as well, but as he was crocked, we weren't unduly concerned.

"WHERE THE FUCK HAVE YOUSE BASTARDS BEEN???"

Our irascible friend was exactly where we'd left him, slumped against the fence, his purple face contorted with fury. The temperature had risen inexorably and he was slowly cooking in the afternoon sun.

"Oh piss off, Hoppy – fuckin' lighten up."

He made a savage lunge towards us, clearly intent on major assault, but merely fell to the ground writhing in pain. His Marty Feldman eyes bulged monstrously.

"WHERE'S MA FUCKING CARRY-OOT?" he demanded, rubbing his swollen ankle fiercely.

"Here," said Irvine, "and I'd just like to say at this point that I think we've all been pretty rotten to you. Slagging a man when he's down. I tell you, it's simply not cricket dear boys!"

"Uh . . . thanks, Irv," said the Orange Liquid Monster gruffly and reluctantly, unused to such pleasantries.

Irvine peeled a can off the plastic holder and held it out. The injured man made a grab for it but missed.

"Whit's the big fucking idea?"

With that, Irvine ripped off the ring pull and took a huge exaggerated slurp out of it, smacking his lips appreciatively. "My, that tastes good! Come and get it then!"

He danced teasingly just out of the injured party's reach, dangling the cans tantalisingly, before skipping back through the site, drinking more of the cans and even giving a couple away to strangers.

The following morning, the car was still in fairly reasonable nick. True, there were several more stains of a Smirnoffian nature, the odd puddle of beer, some refried beans, a muddy footprint or two on the side window, but we were quite proud of ourselves. It's not easy sleeping three to a motor, especially when you're out of your box more or less constantly. When we awoke we listened to the petulant sounds emanating from the adjacent tent.

"There's just *nowhere* to put my make-up on properly!"

"I'm *dying* for a shower!"

"If I don't brush my teeth today I'll go *mad*!"

The rest of the festival passed in the sort of a pleasant haze that epitomises such events at their best. We even managed to catch a few bands. Hawkwind burbled through their time-honoured routine concerning Warriors on the Edge of Time who hide inside in your brain and lurk inside your mind. Truly, the Psychedelic Warlords were born to go as far as they could fly, turning electric dreams into reality . . . or something like that anyway. But did they really perform at all, I asked myself later, after several hash cakes and another litre of Smirnoff? Or did I just imagine it? Who knows? Who cares?

CARSPOTTING

Jethro Tull hit the stage and after three hours of watching the bug-eyed Ian Anderson standing on one leg tootling his flute, I returned to the sleeping quarters. Some time during the night, I was awakened by the sound of someone being loudly and violently ill. Nothing new there and soon I dozed off again. The next morning, however, the true scale of the disaster hit us when we surveyed the interior of our four-wheeled dormitory. In a style that would have impressed Davie in the "Traditional Sunday Breakfast" section of *Trainspotting* (or Spud in the film), Mr Welsh had been picturesquely ill – *indoors.*

We crept from the car like guilty thieves in the night, intending to put as much distance between ourselves and the Strychnine Sisters as possible. They were still asleep, or so we thought. We visited a couple of early-opened stalls, in search of a morning cuppa to soothe the ravaged throats (and nerves). But obtaining a cup of tea at a stall clearly marked "TEA" at such a gathering is not as easy as you might think. The conversation with the stallholder would go like this:

"Cup of tea please?"

". . . tea?"

"Yeah, tea."

"You sure?"

"Uh . . . yes. Quite sure."

"Still got a few tabs of purple moonshine acid left, man!"

"Eh . . . no. Not right now, thanks. Just tea."

"Speed. You wanna buy some whizz?"

"No. I WANT A CUP OF TEA, PLEASE."

". . . how about some Charlie . . .?"

However, we finally scored some far-out Typhoo and then sat around for ages, watching the freaks go by. But our minds were mightily preoccupied. Would we be able to muster up the considerable reserves of courage necessary to return to Strychnine Central? We had to go back at some point, as the tetchy twosome were heading north that day, and as our funds were now just about exhausted, we would have to blag a return ride. The big Hibbie known as Fish was pomp-rocking the night away with his band Marillion the following night but he'd have to do it without us. Eventually we got to our feet and set off, like condemned men heading for the scaffold.

When we approached the scene of the crime, we could see people drifting towards a pile of belongings lying in the mud. Like vultures circling over a dying man in the desert, members of Convoy (the original New Age Travellers) were feasting their beady eyes on what appeared to be a stack of discarded clothes, sleeping bags, cans of beer, bottles of vodka and cameras

"It's funny we can't spot the car from here," remarked Irvine.

"I'm sure it was just ahead," agreed Skinny.

I looked. I looked again. I rubbed my eyes and looked for a third time. A horrible cold feeling gripped the pit of my stomach. Sure enough, when we'd advanced a bit further, we saw all our worldly goods lying unceremoniously in the mire. A set of tyre marks leading away towards the perimeter told their own story.

"YOU STUPID SHIT!!" I howled, jumping up and down in frustration. "It's happened again hasn't it?"

"Eh? What?" stammered Irvine, still not taking in the full picture as it was.

"Well they've only gone and fucked off haven't they? So here we are – *again* – stranded hundreds of miles from home, not a fucking bolt, and so filthy there's no danger we'll be able to hitch. For fuck's sake!" A nearby tent flap unzipped and a shock of hideous orange hair emerged.

"Morning boys," smirked the liquid occupant. "Transport problems?"

Many, many, *many* hours later we found ourselves slumped over a cup of communal tea in a decaying transport café. We watched blearily as the TV news flickered on. It led with footage of 200 riot police charging the New Age Travellers' encampment at Wakefield, up-ending tea stalls with reckless abandon in their frenzied search for illicit substances. I vowed there and then that I would never ever go to another outdoor festival. Never again.

One year later, I came perilously close to drowning, as a tidal wave of mud and raw sewage cascaded through the devastated Glastonbury site. Thunder crashed overhead and rain poured down in raging torrents. At that time, it was the worst ever storm to strike a major festival in the UK – but the show had to go on. And Hawkwind played a blinder, man.

Never say never again . . .?

12

A TEMPORARY ABBERATION

Raining eels and dogs

The Gary Glitter Appreciation Society

Giant greenfly horror in Hackney

"The police were here looking for you," my flatmate informed me one morning.

"What?!"

"You heard."

"Did they say what they wanted?"

"They wanted *you*. Probably with a view to beating your kidneys black and blue with rubber hoses in a small neon-lit brick-lined cell in Oxgangs."

I floated through to the bedroom and hastily packed a bag.

"The Oxgangs Incident" had become a running joke by this time to my acquaintances – had they nothing better to think about? Well, no, obviously. It *was* seven years ago after all, for Christ's sake. There was absolutely no chance that anything was going to come of it now. But the Lothian and Borders Constabulary moved in mysterious ways . . .

In retrospect, the visit was more likely merely a follow-up to a recent unsavoury drama, during which side two of Led Zeppelin's *Physical Graffiti* had been on the turntable at high volume. Everyone had zonked out after mass over-indulgence in a variety of substances, both legal and otherwise, overlooking the fact that the old-fashioned record player just went into repeat mode if left unattended. (Bear in mind that side two features the monster heavy metal stomp of 'Trampled Underfoot' and that mighty booming ascending riff of the classic 'Kashmir'.) So, when the police broke down the door at 5 a.m., we calculated that the neighbours had been subjected to each song approximately *eighteen* times – not to mention 'Houses of the Holy' too, of course.

Ahmed, the mad Egyptian who lived upstairs, had been seriously affected by the disturbance. He frequently ran amok in his bright canary-yellow pyjamas, while waving a wine bottle and screaming that the Israeli Secret Service were going to kill him, and it didn't take much to set him off. Luckily for us, these were rock 'n' roll cops.

"That's Led Zeppelin you know," one of them told Ahmed sternly, as the latter spluttered anti-Semitic sentiments through a mouthful of drool.

"Maybe turn it down a jot," the other said gently. "Sorry about the door. We did try knocking."

But leaving aside all issues with the Constabulary, I just felt like a break anyway. A year or so had elapsed since the last major road trip and in the interval, Irvine had decamped again to London, seemingly on a more permanent basis this time. He'd also acquired a new girlfriend along the way, a development that seemed rather sudden to me but probably only because we hadn't been in touch for a while. What better excuse did I need for a heartfelt visit, principally to express my warmest regards to the happy couple (or my sincerest condolences to the future Mrs Welsh, which would perhaps have been more appropriate)?

At this time, though, there were usually plenty of options open when fleeing to the deep South. A hotchpotch of friends were scattered throughout The Smoke; I decided I might be wiser spreading my presence thinly across a range of floors and settees, so that none of them got *too* sick of me.

Arriving in London after a particularly gruelling 400-mile bitch of a hitch, I planked myself in The Bag O'Nails at Victoria and pondered which Scots ex-pat to call up first. Porno Joe? Robert the Croydon Hibbie? Irvine? I fished out some loose change and headed for the pay phone, wondering how to respond to the inevitable questions from the other end. Like what the fuck are you doing in The Smoke? How long are you staying? Who or what are you running away from? In truth, I had no real concrete answers to any such queries. But I needn't have worried – I drew a blank from all three.

As far as potential sleeping arrangements were concerned, I knew that the railway station was right out of the question. The last time I'd tried to doss down in Victoria, a deranged policeman had driven his car through the main concourse, screaming at the sleeping bagged masses via a loudhailer. Those who failed to respond to demands to LEAVE RIGHT NOW were then kicked awake and tipped headfirst onto the cruel hard ground in a highly effective mopping-up operation. So I spent the night sleeping in a phone box, not a form of shut-eye I would recommend to anyone. If they erected the bastard things on their sides it would have been no problem but I was so shattered I eventually dozed off, crushed into a rough "Z" shape.

The following day – utilising The Bag O'Nails as a base – I continued to seek out free accommodation through my apparently non-existent network of acquaintances resident in the city. At last I got a response from Welsh's number but alas it was not the man himself. A nervous female voice informed me that he had temporarily disappeared. She explained that she occupied the property beneath his and that the phone was situated between the flats. She'd hardly seen him since he'd moved in, bearing only a bed, a fridge and two live eels to his name.

"Two *live eels*?" I demanded with some asperity.

"Uh . . . yes. Two."

I tried to put that to the back of my mind for the moment, wondering where the hell the tenant was.

"I've *no idea* where he is," she reiterated, reading my mind from afar.

"I'll come round anyway," I offered kindly.

"But . . . but . . . I can't let you in if he hasn't come back," she stammered anxiously. "I've got a spare key but, well . . . I don't know who you are, do I?"

"I'm a five-foot-ten Scotsman with long dirty hair, a beard and a Robert Plant T-shirt," I reassured her. "I may be slightly drunk when I get there."

After I'd put the receiver down, I retired to the bar to celebrate over a couple of pints, listening in on a ghastly, soul-destroying conversation between two yuppies about cars, mortgages and Armani suits. In desperation, I flung myself into the company of some Scouse Goths, shamelessly playing the stingy/skint Scots card as they got the drinks in. I left a few hours later in a mellow, slightly tipsy haze, which evaporated completely when I remembered one rather pertinent fact. I didn't have Irvine's address.

After another night in a telephone box, I finally made it as far as Hackney, which at least was the area containing the minimalist nouveau Welsh residence. I knew that much but a fat lot of good it was going to do me, as his downstairs neighbour had now dispensed with her answering service. If he wasn't to be located in the local bars, hospitals or police stations, I really was up shit creek. So I started looking in the pubs, being helped and hindered in about equal parts by some of my fellow countrymen who were in residence in the second boozer. Namely ten bampots originally from Paisley, who were squatting near by.

"We all came doon a couple of years ago, lookin' fur jobs," the one with the glass eye informed me.

"Any luck?"

"Oh aye – we pull jobs all the time," he replied, as his solitary eye winked disconcertingly.

I smiled politely and went back to the nearest pay phone.

A TEMPORARY ABBERATION

This time I finally struck lucky. Welsh had returned and sounded relatively pleased to hear from me.

"Come round now!" he yelled.

By this time, the Paisley jobseekers had offered me alternative accommodation and for a man recently reduced to Telephone Kiosk Doss House Hell, it was nice to have options. I wanted to be sure about one (or rather two) things, however.

"What's all this shit about eels?" I asked sternly.

"Oh – they escaped."

"Are you *sure*?"

I really wasn't sure if my snake phobia extended to eels as well but I suspected that it might. Particularly if hallucinogenic drugs came into the equation. He assured me that Welsh Towers was for the time being an eel-free zone, so I scribbled down the address, bade farewell to Cyclops & Co and headed off for Amhurst Road.

His neighbour had certainly been spot on regarding the furniture situation. The flat contained absolutely nothing other than a bed and a fridge, but as the latter in turn contained a fair cargo of Export cans, the situation was far from bleak. We settled down with backs to the wall, red tins in hand.

"What's happening with the London team then?"

"Nothing much, really. Oh – Stu flung a chair through the window of Barclay's bank last week."

"I see. A political gesture, no doubt?"

"Oh yes. Personal anti-apartheid protest."

"Where did he get the chair from?"

"Well, he was inside the bank at the time you see. He was tapping money off John the Jock, who has an account there. But before John could withdraw any dough, he heard Stu whispering, 'But John, this is *Barclay's* bank!'

" 'So what?' responded John. Then, all of a sudden, there was a huge great fucking *crash* as the glass went in, the alarm went off and everybody dove for cover, with Stu screaming, 'GET OUT OF

125

SOUTH AFRICA YOU RACIST NAZI BASTARDS!' at the top of his voice."

". . . so he never got a loan then?"

"Correct."

I nodded wearily. Finishing off my can, I crawled into my sleeping bag, looking forward with no little trepidation to the next few days. Where Stu was concerned, at least the usual bad behaviour had the virtue of taking on a political hue, but confrontation with Nazi Forces for the State Oppression of the Deprived Proletariat was always a major possibility.

We spent the next few days hanging about The Richmond, which enjoyed similarly liberal licensing hours to those we were used to back home. Not that this was legal south of the border at the time – at 3 p.m., they simply locked you in for a couple of hours minimum. It was peopled by pool sharks, "loveable" villains and Stu's Rastafarian neighbours, who had yet to undergo political indoctrination. But that was on the agenda, he assured us. It emerged that Stu had also recently been caught in the company of his gangsterish sidekick Mel, as they attempted to break into premises in the City one night – "for political reasons", predictably enough. In fact, Stu had been caught red-handed with a politically incorrect crowbar in his hands, levering the door off its hinges. His Redistribution of Wealth theories had subsequently failed to win the hearts and minds of the boys from the Met.

At some point during all this nonsense, Welsh's pet crisis escalated. His girlfriend (and wife-to-be) thoughtfully purchased him a puppy to replace the missing eels. As I was with her at the time, I was later branded an accessory to this piece of foolishness. I had seldom seen Irvine at a loss for words but his face as he beheld the excitable creature charging frantically about his pad, shitting everywhere, spoke volumes. Following the lead of his literary hero, William S. Burroughs, he thoroughly disapproved of the beasts.

A TEMPORARY ABBERATION

The "Deid Dugs" chapter in *Trainspotting* had more than a touch of wishful thinking about it, where this unlikely cat-lover – and one-time owner of the felines known as Fish-Breath and Shit-Tray – was concerned. His hatred of canines stemmed from his days spent working for Park Patrol, when any errant dog owner allowing his pet to foul the hallowed turf of Inverleith Park was in turn foully abused by the irate parkie. A stream of complaints to Head Office finally put the mockers on that particular promising career.

Anyway, he proceeded to deal with his live dug torment by deciding to camp out with myself at Mel's place for a while.

"I canny stand any more of that incessant barking!" he declared, his face screwed up in misery as we chapped at Mel's door. "I *hate* dugs!"

There was an ominous pattering of (large) feet followed by a deafening fusillade of enraged barking, as some beast of Baskerville Hound proportions crashed into the door from the other side. Irvine leapt like a startled gazelle. I took a couple of hasty steps back as Mel cautiously opened the door on its chain, revealing a slavering-jawed Alsatian literally straining at the leash to rip the two Jock intruders limb from limb.

The mind-boggling stupidity of simply swapping one dog pound for another (with a far larger and fiercer dog) shows just how fucked up our heads were at this point. There was also the slightly troubling factor that this dog's owner reeked so strongly of major-league criminality that he might as well have been wearing a suit with arrows embroidered on it.

"His bark's worse than 'is bite, innit?" observed Mel unconvincingly, as we filed nervously past Al. Well, that turned out to be true but the same could not have been said of his wife. She kept us awake until 5 a.m. barking all sorts of unlikely tales in our direction, about her life and times dahn the East End in the good ol' days. It was like being shut in a room with an incessantly jabbering radio tuned to some mercilessly high frequency that you couldn't switch off.

Oh Gawd, she'd known 'em all, hadn't she? Well probably not. The Krays, Mad Frankie Fraser, Jack the Hat . . . I'd already spent two nights struggling to sleep in a phone-box, one on Irv's bare floorboards having nightmares about eels in my sleeping bag, one on Stu's settee as the Revolution gathered momentum around me, one half-suffocated in dope smoke at Errol the Rastafarian's, but I could tell that this was going to be the most trying yet. Especially since I had to share the couch with Al the dog (the Alsatian was *de rigueur* amongst your average East End crim in those days, before Rottweillers and pit-bulls became trendy). But I finally passed out, as gentle dreams of Reg and Ron torturing victims in dimly lit snooker halls played through my subconscious mind. Or was that just those wimps from Spandau Ballet in the movie . . .?

There was one final unpleasant surprise regarding sleeping arrangements up ahead but I wasn't to know that as we struck out for The Richmond in the morning. Our personal EastEnders soap opera was already gathering pace, as we eased our way past Al and the rest of Mel's improvised security systems. Sadly, it was unlike the good ol' days dahn the manor, when everyone left their doors unlocked and you could hardly get moving for the Kray twins helping old ladies across the road. Or so we were told anyway.

We spent most of the day in the boozer, before heading round to Stu's to check on the latest situation regarding the Overthrow of the Establishment. But the man was too busy throwing Carlsberg Specials down his neck to be bothered. We sociably produced our familiar red tins, just as Amphetamine Arthur dropped by with further items designed to put a zip in our step. Eventually, fired up on an unhealthy and dangerous cocktail of various substances, we decided to hit the street. Errol and Arthur were too lazy to progress beyond The Richmond, however, which left myself, Irv and Stu to seek out the high spots of Stoke Newington.

A TEMPORARY ABBERATION

We were fortunate to avoid a stomping quite early on, in a grim bar as we listened to an even grimmer Country & Western act, fronted by "The Legendary Bobby Katt". We applauded each song wildly, until it began to dawn slowly but surely on the C&W hordes that our cheers bore somewhat sarcastic overtones. Then again, it was hard to tell in Irvine's case. Was he merely taking the piss or was he actually *enjoying* this sugar-coated syrupy shite? A man whose record collection boasted works by such artists as Boney M, The Bay City Rollers, Barry Blue and Engelbert Humperdink was never to be trusted musically, I felt.

We succeeded in leaving without a kicking, having pushed our luck quite far enough. A growl of disapproval followed us as we skedaddled in an exaggeratedly nonchalant manner. I half-expected a posse of Stetson-sporting cowboy types to follow us out and smoke us down like dogs in the gutter. After all, it's not every day you witness a loud beer-spilling Scotsman, a long-haired-hippy faggot type and a shady-looking black anarchist abusing the locals in a hoedown hangout.

From there on, things progressed in the standard downhill manner. We reeled from pub to pub. Then, the most unpredictable of drugs reared its ugly head, i.e. whisky. At closing time, we poured ourselves out into the street, "singing" vociferously. The noise was admittedly more consistent with one of the feline species being strangled in a vocal style not a million miles away from that of the appropriately named Mr Robert Katt. Dustbins and other items of urban flotsam and jetsam that impeded our progress soon wound up being merrily kicked into touch. And all the while, the merits of Hibernian and West Ham United football clubs were loudly proclaimed in musical verse. So it was not entirely surprising that the much-feared Stoke Newington constabulary soon arrived at the scene, telling us pointedly to shut the fuck up and behave. This only made matters worse.

The previous week, London police officers had accidentally

gunned down an innocent motorist whilst hunting for the escaped transvestite gunman David Martin and, by this time, the reverberations of their reckless behaviour were beginning to sound far and wide (even our local Starsky and Hutch boys baulked at blowing away law abiding citizens in broad daylight). This then was the cue for some sudden inspiration from Welsh's lips.

"YOU SHOT THE WRONG MAN, YOU SHOT THE WRONG MAN, HALLO!" he shrieked, in parody of the old Gary Glitter foot-stomper, jabbing an accusing finger at the grim-faced bobbies. Myself and Stu took up the cry enthusiastically. It *was* quite catchy, after all. Many hands roughly seized us from all directions. The unpleasant if not exactly unfamiliar sensation of being bundled unceremoniously into the back of a police car was upon us once more. At the station, they flung us in a large cell, mainly populated by black guys who looked like archetypal street dope dealers. They seemed somewhat alarmed at the noise that accompanied our entrance to their sleeping quarters.

"YOU SHOT THE WRONG MAN, YOU SHOT THE WRONG MAN!" Irvine reiterated, as the heavy steel door slammed behind us. It was lucky that Stu was on hand to confide in me the reason why we'd been arrested. It was a racist inspired set-up apparently.

"It's because I'm black and you and Irv are Scottish," he explained. He then moved to a position level with the grille on the door – which Irvine had just vacated – and emitted a long, loud, blood-curdling scream.

"SHUT UP!!" roared an irate voice of Authority from down the passage.

Stu repeated his performance. As the heavy clump of boots came down the corridor, I hastily curled up in a ball, pretending to be asleep. But the cop just stuck his face threateningly up against the grille and reinforced his view that we should "SHUT THE FUCK UP, OR ELSE . . ." The rest was left to our imagination. Unpleasant thoughts flooded through our booze-sodden brains, as only recently an arrested youth had died in mysterious circumstances in the very same cells. More subtle tactics were clearly called for.

"I KNOW MY RIGHTS, I KNOW MY RIGHTS! I DEMAND TO MAKE A PHONE CALL!!"

Even I jumped as Welsh's dulcet tones pierced the brief silence with eardrum-bursting force. By this time, the other occupants of the cell had moved away to a corner and were observing our behaviour with great concern. Irvine repeated his request. A cursing policeman eventually complied, probably under the impression that a lawyer was going to be contacted. He seemed to want rid of us as soon as possible.

"IT'S NONE OF YOUR BUSINESS WHO I PHONE! I KNOW MY RIGHTS! I DEMAND TO . . ."

Welsh's harangue continued as he was led away in the direction of the telephone. All was quiet for about thirty seconds. Then came the distant, yet unmistakable sound of a telephone receiver being slammed down furiously, with a cry of ". . . AND WE'LL DO YOU FOR WASTING POLICE TIME TOO, YOU JOCK BASTARD!!"

Myself and Stu watched with interest as Irvine reappeared, a policeman's thumb and forefinger attached to his ear. The door was opened and he was flung violently back into the cell. For all of half a minute, I had been genuinely contemplating trying to sleep, but it was now obviously going to be out of the question.

"YOU SHOT THE WRONG MAN, YOU SHOT THE . . ."

"What happened then?" I demanded, more to shut him up temporarily that anything else.

"*What happened*?" he shouted incredulously. "The bastards only went and SHOT THE WRONG MAN, that's what happened!"

"No. What happened *just now*?"

It transpired that once reaching the telephone, inspiration had failed him. Memory of any useful numbers for legal contacts had failed too. So he phoned an old mate in Muirhouse, Edinburgh, to inform him conversationally that we'd been arrested for staging a protest about police brutality, which was a damned disgrace and no mistake. Tommo – possibly as a result of being woken out of a deep sleep in the early hours of the morning by a drunken maniac from his past – showed little interest in our predicament.

We in turn were awoken brutally several hours later, with no offer of breakfast forthcoming. Yet I could hardly complain. Despite still being drunk, I realised that during my stay in London, I'd had by far the best sleep that night. The mattresses provided by Stoke Newington crimebusters ensured a level of comfort that had been sadly lacking up until this point. Phone-boxes, floors and settees were comprehensively put to shame.

We were ushered upstairs to collect our trouser-belts and shoelaces. The surly desk sergeant rounded furiously on Welsh, who was rocking to and fro on his heels and laughing quietly to himself.

"*So you think this is all a big laugh then do you?*" he shouted.

The guilty party's ongoing chuckling indicated that he probably did.

Quivering with fury, the irascible man pointed at the door marked "Exit" (which was made of glass and virtually indistinguishable from the surrounding plate-glass window). "Now FUCK OFF out of it and mind you don't walk into the . . ."

There was a terrible crash and I reeled back absolutely stunned, almost knocking myself unconscious as I walked straight into the window. The glass bulged and vibrated alarmingly. As did my forehead. I staggered about half-concussed, clasping my bleeding head in my hands. Welsh roared with delight at my misfortune as we were roughly hustled outside, with bits of paper clutched in our shaky hands. On closer inspection, these invited us to Old Street Magistrates' Court in approximately one week's time for further entertainment.

A TEMPORARY ABBERATION

THE TRIAL
Good morning Worm your honour
The crown will plainly show
The prisoner who now stands before you
Was caught red handed showing feelings
Showing feelings of an almost human nature
Shame on him
This will not do

What has happened to me is only a single instance and as such of no great importance, especially as I do not take it very seriously, but it is representative of a misguided policy which is being directed against many other people as well. It is for these that I take up my stand here, not for myself.

I had only been in court twice before, on both occasions as a mere spectator. But now it was different. It was eight days later and I was back in London again. I had hitched all the way up that bloody 373-mile-long Road to the North, only to virtually turn right round and thumb it all the way back down again, or at least that's the way it seemed at the time. Time! Now there's an ominous word . . .

I awoke groggily on Irvine's floor on the Monday morning, wondering what kind of mood he would be in. In my absence, he had been going through a sort of Tortured Artist phase, which involved sitting around launderettes looking pale and interesting, wearing a long black coat while listlessly slugging from a bottle of Grouse. However, he was now in animation mode, striding around the room encased in a dark blue suit with shoes brightly polished and a reflective gleam in his eye.

"Here's how we play it," he announced in a brisk business–like voice.

"I take the part of the city whizz-kid who has overstepped the mark unintentionally while over-indulging, celebrating the conclusion of some Big Deal. But I'm man enough to admit I've been a naughty boy. Loads of remorse and all that crap. No! I've got it! It was the night of my engagement! Yes, that's it, you and Stu – work colleagues – were helping me on my way to the altar! Someone spiked my drinks maybe . . .? Business rivals . . ."

I eyed him fearfully. Pale-and-interesting was preferable to this. Somehow the vision of three whisky-crazed hooligans of dubious ethnic origins singing football songs and screaming their heads off about mistaken shootings while viciously booting dustbins about did not square with the image of yuppies on a night out.

"Are you sure this is a good idea?" I ventured, reluctantly crawling out of my sleeping bag. "You know what happened last time you tried to get funny in court after Wembley."

"This is a different ball game altogether. Same rules do not apply. Eh . . . what happened at Wembley again?"

"You got fined twice as much as everyone else who got lifted for being a smart-arse."

"Oh aye . . ."

Some time later, our dragging footfalls could have been heard, echoing through the depressing streets as we plodded half-heartedly towards the court. We had called in for Stu, who was in a doubly gloomy mood, as he was on a six-month suspended sentence for "revolutionary" crimes at the time.

"They'll put me away for this one," he forecasted dolefully.

Mel had been apprehended by the Long Arm of the Law the previous week and it could be fairly said that our current predicament positively paled into insignificance when set alongside his. (He later got a fifteen-year stretch – for armed robbery.)

We passed a traditional fishmongers', which had a basin of eels on display outside. Irvine brightened up briefly and shot me a wistful glance. I shook my head firmly. The ramifications caused by

Fox (drinking) and Irvine (cool shades), at Bob Dylan's Blackbushe Picnic, 1978

(Left to right) Irvine, Lassie, Afghan Ali and Willie in The Western Bar

The Orange Liquid Monster: a truly terrible human being

Hangin' with the hippies in Nicolson Street – (left to right) Rocky, Burglar-Alarm Steve, Ali B, Tam, Irvine and Mad Al (front)

Rocky with the Crazy Cannabis Cop of Wakefield

The author (left) and Irvine (centre) enjoy a quiet night in with Evil Ertch (right)

Irv in his PVC breeks, with Cowgirl Linda and Evil Ertch at the Nite Club

The late Alg, one of the good guys, 1983

Don't mess with this mob, matey! Broken-down Angels on the road to Glastonbury – (left to right) Tank, Stonewall (kneeling), Stine and Rustler

Irvine acquires an Aberdeen scarf at Jambo Jill's New Year party

Stu and the author plot revolution in The Richmond

Mail bonding: with fellow postie, Anita

Christmas time with Irvine at Ryries

The author (centre) outside Brendan Behan's old local, and scene of literary decadence down the decades

"I'll f*****g bacon roll ye in a minute!" – Maggie

Irv in his Leith pad with Stan the Bam

Booze Brother Roddy MacKenzie would later form the Jerry Garcia influenced Dreadful Grate tribute band

"'zine of the times" – Promo shot for the *Hibs Monthly* magazine

The author, with Hibernian FC legend Pat Stanton, at Irvine's *Ecstasy* launch

With Irvine in Glasgow before the ill-fated League Cup Final of 2004

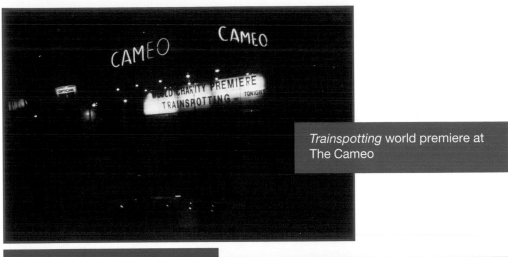

Trainspotting world premiere at The Cameo

Fox chats to Robert "Begbie" Carlyle, as the Librarian smirks in the foreground

Trainspotting director Danny Boyle with the Librarian

Fox with Irvine at the latter's engagement do at Robbie's Bar, Leith. No snakes were harmed during the making of this shirt

Flanked by Irvine and Fox in Robbie's Bar

With Mrs and Mr Welsh at The Spider's Web

wriggling sea creatures let loose within the solemn portals of Old Street Magistrates' court would not help our situation, I deduced brilliantly.

As last we reached the building and then had to kick our heels for a while before being called in. Irvine strode to and fro impatiently, eager to get into his "wronged yuppie" routine. Then our names were called and we entered the vast legal bowl, which was packed to the gunnels. I shuddered inwardly with imminent stage fright.

The first case we witnessed did nothing to alter Stu's pessimistic predictions. An expensively groomed Turkish guy was up for drunk-driving and the magistrate lost no time in throwing the book at him from every possible angle. He pulled £100 fines out of the air for trifling technicalities like they were going out of fashion. The hapless victim was driven into the ground by a succession of these. His confident demeanour fell apart like a house of cards as the beak rained words of fire and brimstone down on him like a medieval preacher. He left the dock actually *weeping*. Oh shit! Was that to be our ignominious fate too?

Next on the bill were two prostitutes.

"I see you have fourteen previous convictions for soliciting," he remarked to one. "The last one was in Birmingham two weeks ago. When did you arrive in London?"

"Friday," she replied.

"Well, I advise you be out of London by *next* Friday *at the latest*. Fined £200."

Holy fuck. But luckily the next two acts on the programme actually seemed to put him in a good mood. The first gentleman he recognised instantly.

"Mr Hussey! That's every Monday *this year* we've seen you in this court. What was it this time? Ahh! Surely not drunk and incapable again. Fined £5."

"Thank you, your honour!" grovelled the debonair Mr Hussey

urbanely, before shuffling out in a raincoat that smelled like an overflowing cesspit.

"Brazen hussy, all right," I whispered to Welsh but he didn't respond. His eyes were like gimlets, all thoughts concentrated towards the main act. Hussey's co-star was a fellow archetypal piss-artist, who explained that he'd been suffering from blackouts and had therefore drunk a whole bottle of whisky "t'see if it would clear me head yer honour". His tentative advances in alternative medical science cost him a fiver too. But now it was time for the main action . . .

Some ten days ago I was arrested, in a manner that seems ridiculous even to myself, though that is immaterial at the moment. The whole matter has caused me nothing but some unpleasantness and passing annoyance, but might it not have had *worse* consequences?

© 1925 from *The Trial* by Franz Kafka

The evidence before the court is
Incontrovertible, there's no need for
The jury to retire
In all my years of judging
I have never heard before of
Some one more deserving
The full penalty of the law
The way you made them suffer
Your exquisite wife and mother
Fills me with the urge to defecate
But my friend you have revealed
Your deepest fear
I sentence you to be exposed before
Your peers
Tear down the wall.

Copyright © 1979 'The Trial' by Roger Waters

A TEMPORARY ABBERATION

I gave my account first, explaining that I was just an innocent lad from the North, caught up unawares in the vice and corruption of the big city and exposed to the ravages of the demon drink (which I wasn't used to) etc., all the time being uncomfortably aware that my appearance (combat jacket, same old Rab Plant T-shirt, hair, beard and so on) was loudly screaming "BULLSHIT! GUILTY AS CHARGED AND OFF WITH HIS HEAD" to the rafters. I was almost knocked out of my stride as Irvine gave a snort of derision/laughter at one point, which he unsuccessfully tried to disguise as a cough.

"Mmmmm," said the magistrate eloquently, observing me over his rimless spectacles. "Yes, I see your address here is given as 'Edinburgh'. So you will doubtless have incurred considerable expenditure in getting here, rail fares being what they are?"

"Eh? Rail f—— Oh yes, yes indeed your honour," I gabbled, almost blowing it.

I had doubtless incurred considerable expenditure, but that was through buying Yorkie bars and even the occasional transport café meal for various hitch-hiker-friendly lorry drivers, as well as copious amounts of booze.

His gaze moved along the line and came to rest on the Man in the Dark Blue Suit.

"Mr Welsh. How do you plead, guilty or not . . ."

"GUILTY!!!" barked back Irvine, in a Sergeant-Major-On-Parade voice, causing myself, Stu and the rest of the court to jump in alarm.

"Ahh. Anything else to say . . .?"

Welsh promptly launched into his "foolish whizz-kid with one too many gin and tonics" spiel, spewing out long-winded claptrap of the most nauseating kind. He spoke in hushed tones about the disgrace he had brought down on his hard-working, God-fearing, law-abiding family. Even the magistrate was beginning to look bored when he concluded his statement, summing up the whole sorry affair as being "just a temporary aberration your honour".

Stu then played a low-key role by his standards, trying to look as abject and humble as possible. He failed. He just looked like a violent left-wing revolutionary black anarchist who would torch the whole building at the first possible opportunity. But the suspended sentence hanging over him had seemingly taken the wind out of his sails, which was just as well. The whole charade was merely a racist-inspired inquisition anyway, in his opinion, and thus beneath contempt.

We waited with bated breath for the verdict.

"Taking into account all the facts of this case," boomed the Voice of Doom, "I am inclined to agree with Mr Welsh that this was merely a *temporary aberration*. Conditionally discharged to be of good behaviour for six months."

Our collective expression of open-mouthed surprise was matched only by the attendant polis' collective expression of open-mouthed fury. We fell out of the court in a daze.

"Welsh does it again!" yelled the erstwhile City Whizz-Kid in delight, alarming one of the ladies of the night who'd been charged earlier, as she strutted past us drinking a can of Super Lager. "Welsh gets the boys off the hook! Did you hear him? He agreed with *me*! 'I am inclined to agree with Mr Welsh that this was merely a TEMPORARY ABBERATION!'"

It was not long before Irv's joy at his own cleverness reached such unbearable proportions that I half-wished we had been flung in the slammer (but one with comfy beds, mind you).

That evening we purchased *The Hackney Gazette* to see if the non-permanent aberration had been duly reported and discovered that, unfortunately, we'd missed the star turn. On being asked why he'd broken into his neighbour's house while drunk, naked and brandishing a large axe, the defendant yelled back that "THE BASTARD HAD BEEN PUTTING GIANT GREENFLY IN

A TEMPORARY ABBERATION

MY CENTRAL HEATING SYSTEM AGAIN!!!" Another temporary aberration? The magistrate certainly seemed to think so and merely referred him for psychiatric treatment.

"*Giant greenfly!*" yelled Irvine in undisguised admiration.

We then hit the mean streets of Hackney, recklessly throwing around the money we'd put aside for the fines that had miraculously failed to materialise. Whisky entered the equation fairly early on. In fact, our celebrations resulted in exactly the same sort of behaviour that had got us lifted in the first place.

The next day, I wearily set off on another wretched, soul-destroying, 373-mile trek, reflecting sadly on the cruel horrors of Life As We Know It. A temporary aberration it may have been but how many days or weeks would elapse before another one occurred? Being acquainted with Welsh was once again at the root of my problems. And being acquainted with Welsh is a *permanent* aberration.

ALBERT KIDD

Bonnie Dundee

Up against the wall motherfuckers!

There's a riot goin' on

Pogue mahone

After the dust had settled slightly over the latest London adventure, I found myself alone in the flat one day, wielding a black marker pen and a sizeable sheet of white cardboard. Slowly and deliberately, I took up the pen and wrote the following on the white background: DO NOT RETURN TO LONDON AGAIN FOR ANY REASON.

I stood back to admire my handiwork and felt that there was perhaps something missing. A mental light bulb flashed on in my head and I changed the full stop to a comma before adding: PARTICULARLY IF IT INVOLVES WELSH IN ANY SHAPE OR FORM. That was better. After all, what on earth was the point in running away from the Edinburgh polis when any encounter with their Metropolitan brethren was guaranteed to be at least twice as traumatic? I placed this piece of minimalist artwork on the mantelpiece, where I could hardly avoid seeing it, and vowed to heed its message. I was repeating the mantra under my breath when the telephone rang.

"The bastards are going to do it, aren't they? The bastards are going to actually win the fucking league!"

I nodded dumbly at the sound of Irvine's distraught voice crackling down the wires from London. Having just watched Dundee United throw in the towel and lose 3-0 at home to Hearts on television, I had to concur with this unpalatable possibility. But hope in Hibbies' hearts had been ebbing away for weeks now, as our city rivals had piled 1-0 victory upon 1-0 victory. Now, with this resounding win, they looked virtually unstoppable in their demented charge towards the Premier League title of 1986.

In the usual childish manner of soccer saddoes, we had spent the previous thirteen years casting up Hibs' famous 7-0 win on New Year's Day 1973 at Tynecastle to Hearts followers wherever we could find them. As we drank in a staunch Hearts pub at the time (The Diggers, just a stone's throw from Hearts' Tynecastle stadium), they weren't exactly hard to find. And like the Boer War adversaries of Corporal Jones in *Dad's Army*, they didn't like it up 'em – not one little bit. So I realised with a sinking feeling that that was all about to change. The gloating that would accompany Hearts' first trophy-winning success in about 300 years would be absolutely unbearable. Even worse, acquaintances of mine who had never previously exhibited any interest in the Beautiful Game had taken to swanning around in brand new maroon-and-white favours, desperate to ride the bandwagon whilst they could. There was clearly only one course of action open to me. I would have to leave the country immediately.

However, plans to get as far away from Edinburgh as possible (Tibet was pencilled in as a possible destination) ran into the ground as soon as myself and two fellow escapees stopped off in the capital city of that strange land adjoining our own. We simply couldn't get out of it again. The social quagmire that surrounded Welsh and his entourage was entirely to blame for this. Before we knew it, the day we were dreading rolled around, as we lay there on Porno Joe's floor idly perusing the latest additions to his Library of Obscenity.

Dens Park, Dundee, was where the unthinkable was due to occur in a few hours' time. The home team were no great shakes and there was little doubt that Hearts – with a run of over thirty unbeaten games to their credit – would emerge triumphant. Even if they lost, Celtic would need to score a barrow-load in their game away to St Mirren to overhaul the leaders on goal difference. I tried to take my mind off things by concentrating on *Hot-Blooded Dutch Tailors* but to no avail.

As usual, the delicate mechanism of my body clock had suffered a spanner being rudely chucked in its works by Irvine. His infuriating habit of leading us on a succession of Welsh wild goose chases had continued unabated, dragging us mile after mile across the city to late opening clubs and other sundry dives, which would turn out to not open late at all or not exist in the first place.

I always found riding the Underground a depressing and exhausting business anyway, dodging pickpockets, assorted bampots and high quality beggars of Glaswegian origin. Then there was the usual series of impromptu all night parties at a variety of locations, with the attendant risk of confrontation with police officers summoned by irate neighbours. This meant we would generally awaken on someone's floor in the afternoon, before heading out for breakfast-cum-lunch-cum-dinner. All the people I seemed to know in London were adept at keeping their homes well stocked with booze, drugs, pornography and illegal weaponry, but food storage appeared to be an alien concept. I left the Dutch tailors to their own unspeakable devices and joined my fellow dossers, who were heading out for sustenance.

As we sat in a greasy Brixton café trying to digest something strange and unidentifiable at around 3.30, we became aware of the indistinct voice emanating from the radio behind the counter. This came from a sports announcer, who was muttering something about Dundee taking a 1-0 lead. As such, it wasn't much to get excited about, bearing in mind the frequent inability of English pundits to differentiate between Dundee and Dundee United (and indeed this score turned out to be incorrect, but we weren't to know it at the time). However, Evil Ertch leapt up like he'd been plugged into the mains and stung by a swarm of bees simultaneously, knocking over cups and saucers in his agitation.

"Turn it up! TURN IT UP!" he yelled at the poor woman behind the counter, who looked terrified, but duly obliged. Even then, rumours were starting to filter through about Celtic cracking them in at Love Street but with the reportage focusing almost entirely on the English championship race, nothing was very clear.

We dived out of the café post-haste and raced back to Porno Joe's, where the diminutive filth-hoarder swiftly put aside *Ice Maidens of Stockholm* and demanded to know the reason for all the hysteria. "Hearts are getting gubbed!" shrieked Evil Ertch.

"Maybe," I cautioned.

"Maybe not," retorted Brixton's premier purveyor of continental glossy magazines. "At half time it was 0-0."

"What!"

"According to the TV anyway."

"Shite! How about Celtic?"

"Look," said our host irritably, "I don't *care* about Celtic. I care even *less* about Hearts. I've told you all many times that Dunfermline Athletic are the only team worth bothering about. The Pars have a long illustrious history, during which . . ."

His flow of speech was abruptly halted as Welsh pitched a well-thumbed copy of *Almost Too Big* at him and I switched the TV back on. But predictably, all the talk was of Liverpool and Everton.

We spent the next hour or so in an agony of suspense. Viewing Rugby-bloody-League was never my idea of a good way to pass an afternoon and never less so than now, as I stared frantically at the screen, my face a churning sea of apprehension. I realised it was absolutely pathetic of course, this deranged desire to see unexpected misfortune descend on what were, to a large extent, inhabitants of our home town. But that did nothing to dilute the feeling. Far from it. After interminable footage of fifteen-stone boneheads rucking about in the mud, the picture changed and some familiar-looking Brylcreemed muppet swam into view. He wore that slightly alien look that is the trademark of the Scottish football presenter. The screen then cut to footage of some initially unidentified ground, where hordes of green-, white- and yellow-clad people were dancing on the pitch. Cue the commentator's hysterical tones: ". . . and incredible scenes here in Paisley, where, against *all* odds, Celtic have clinched . . ."

That night, the partying surpassed anything that had gone before. In the days before "London Hibs" became an official entity, a loose aggregation of Easter Road expatriates would occasionally gather under the banner of "The Essex and East London Hibs Supporters Club" (or so Irvine claimed, but I suspected that they merely consisted of himself and Robert the Croydon Hibbie). If so, the entire membership was certainly up for it that night.

Robert was a top-ranking civil servant who enjoyed the quiet life in the South – or at least he had done, until Welsh became his near neighbour. It was amazing how even the most conservative of people could be led astray by Irv, as was proved by a bizarre incident that had occurred not long before. For reasons that were never made entirely clear, the pair had been apprehended by hotel security while masquerading as Australian rock stars, as they attacked shocked guests in the corridors of a five-star establishment with well aimed jets of water from fire hoses. Welsh seemed to labour under the delusion that his former incarnation as a shite punk guitarist gave him the right to indulge in archetypal rock 'n' roll behaviour as the fancy took him.

But the climax to what would be forever after referred to as "Albert Kidd Day" (in honour of the player who scored the two goals that broke Hearts in Dundee), was possibly even more eventful. We had piled into Mrs Welsh's car at pub closing time, in search of more action. Anne had not long passed her test and was particularly nervous as 1) the car was full of screaming drunks, 2) it was horribly overcrowded, containing *seven* of the aforementioned inebriates, namely myself, Irvine, Fox, Porno Joe, Stu, Amphetamine Arthur, Evil Ertch and, of course, the driver, and 3) two of the passengers were in possession of sufficient quantities of illegal drugs which – if we were intercepted by the police – would see us banged up in Wormwood Scrubs until Hearts next nearly won the league. In other words, for a very long time. As Welsh had the window wound down and was bawling unintelligible gibberish at passers-by, this seemed not entirely unlikely. And the next suggestion from Stu made it almost inevitable.

This was that we should detour via Rupert Murdoch's News International plant at Wapping, where nightly picketing by strikers had been getting increasingly more violent. As was common in London, all sorts of other bedsit revolutionaries, anarchists and anti-social maniacs with their own political or personal agendas had joined their ranks. People just like Stu, in fact. But we had to show solidarity with our oppressed brethren in the proletarian struggle, he informed us sternly. Welsh carried on screaming out of the window. Myself, Fox and Evil Ertch carried on stoically drinking. Arthur carried on popping pills. Anne and Porno Joe carried on looking like they wished they were somewhere else entirely.

Although Irvine's revolutionary credentials were in no way comparable to Stu's, he had idly dabbled in anarchy in the UK, or in Cramond Village to be precise. As a disciple of some Muirhouse freedom fighter with psychiatric problems, he would occasionally be ordered to hurl the odd petrol bomb at a tree with a target painted on it. But that was when he'd been much younger and foolish. Now that he was older and foolish, however, it still gave him a cheap thrill when the first home-made bomb flew past our vehicle with a WHOOOOOSH and exploded against a parked car, setting it ablaze picturesquely beneath the night sky.

It appeared that we had arrived at Wapping. The air was filled with the angry, confused roar that a huge uncontrollable mob makes when it's uncertain who to put to the sword next. Stu let out a whoop of joy. Anne had fearfully slowed the car down and we were almost at a halt anyway when the policeman appeared out of nowhere, his hand raised ominously in a "STOP" gesture. Ten years at least, I thought. With no parole.

Our driver appeared frozen in shock and just managed to bring the car under control before it collided with the size twelve boots. Luckily her husband had stopped screaming just in time and it was Anne's turn to wind her window down as the Law loomed up before us.

"You can't go through this way," he stated firmly.

Well, as an opening line, it certainly beat, "Do you mind if I search your passengers?" I reasoned.

"Wh—why not?" responded Anne timidly.

He sighed. As the sky was lit up like bonfire night, with petrol bombs arching through the air, he probably thought it was obvious.

"There's a riot going on . . ."

". . . up in cell block No. 9," added Irvine rashly.

The cop's demeanour changed instantly and he glared suspiciously in at the car's occupants for the first time. Here it comes, I thought. "*Up against the wall motherfuckers* but you have the right to remain silent . . ." However, he just indicated that we would have to turn round and return the way we had come.

Anne desperately manoeuvred around in the confusing darkness. Apart from the occasional flare from petrol bombs some 100 yards away, it was virtually pitch dark, as a lot of streetlights had apparently been smashed earlier.

Now we had additional complications, as Stu and Arthur wanted to be let off nearer the scene of protest. I just wanted to go back to Irvine's or Porno Joe's and drink beer. Fox and Evil Ertch wanted huge amounts of Indian food. Porno Joe wanted nothing more than a chance to curl up with a good book, of the "Not to be Sold to Minors" variety. Welsh apparently wanted "a man after midnight", if his enthusiastic rendering of the Abba classic was to be taken at face value. However, next minute, our preferences were rendered entirely superfluous. Anne turned a corner and accelerated forward – right into the midst of one of the worst riots of the decade.

The air throbbed with sound and fury, as police horses snickered wildly and thundered through the baying mob, completely out of control. Glass smashed relentlessly as a never-ending stream of petrol bombs soared towards the police lines and scary, demented looking people, smeared in blood, charged around with scaffolding poles and other makeshift weapons. The sky was obscured by thick palls of smoke, through which golf balls, paving slabs and other missiles rained down. Even through the firmly closed windows, we could hear the terrible screams of people being trampled underfoot, as a woman with a shopping trolley raised above her bloodied head fell against the bonnet. It was clearly a time for stout hearts and brave deeds. For courage and valour. How would the contemporary heroes of our violent age have responded? What would Albert Kidd have done?

We eventually got out of the inferno by pure luck, i.e. by Anne accelerating away from the mayhem at top speed and to fuck with anyone unlucky enough to get in the way. The angry roar diminished to a mere whisper on the horizon as we put as much distance between ourselves and Rupert Murdoch's personal Alamo as possible. I now understood only too well the concept of "newspaper wars". But our oppressed brethren would have to make do without us this time around. We hastened back to Irvine's and proceeded to consume large quantities of whisky until 6 a.m.

Around this time, our host decided that it might be a good idea to telephone as many Hearts-supporting acquaintances as he could, to offer sincerest condolences. The astronomical level of rage expressed by a "Jambo Begbie", who was called up anonymously, was such that we all quaked in our boots, despite being 400 miles away.

On awakening in the late morning, we learned that we had indeed experienced the worst night of violence at Wapping so far, with over 300 police officers injured. Stu *had* been a busy boy.

Predictably, the television and newspapers made little reference to the casualties on the other side. Disgracefully, even *less* mention was made of Albert Kidd's heroics, but we had that to look forward to on returning north of the border. There wasn't much excuse for hiding out in The Smoke any longer, now that the awful threat of Jambo jubilation had been lifted.

Foolishly, though, we did stay on to take in a folk festival, which was set to be staged in St George's Park. The Pogues were meant to be headlining but then lead singer Shane MacGowan managed to get himself run over whilst drunk some nights before. So they pulled out. The whole event had been badly promoted – if at all – and the attendance numbered in the hundreds rather than the thousands, who might reasonably have been expected to turn up had the Boys From County Hell put in an appearance. Still, it was nice and peaceful lying there with Fox and Evil Ertch in the afternoon sunshine. Welsh had poured withering scorn on the whole shebang and taken himself off to the boozer.

So, when a rumpus developed at the entrance to the site, we paid little attention at first. It continued to grow in intensity and more and more people became distracted as the police presence around the fence started to multiply rapidly. We took a closer look – and recoiled instantly in alarm. Irvine and Stu – completely out of their heads and armed with objects that looked suspiciously like scaffolding poles – were attempting to gatecrash. As the former hadn't wanted to go in the first place, I surmised that he'd been roped into these antics by Stu, who was obviously still on a high after attempting to overthrow the Murdoch Empire the previous evening. Truly, the People's Revolution never slept. But what political objective could be attained by storming a gathering of Men With Beards (and fingers in their ears singing "Hey Nonny No") was beyond me. As they were repelled by the thin blue line, I heard Irvine defiantly yell something about Albert Kidd.

The following day, we returned to Edinburgh and dropped in at The Diggers for a pint. It occurred to me for the first time that Glaswegians are spot on when they complain that Edinburgh folk are stuck-up and unfriendly. For some reason, no one would speak to us.

CRY CROSSROADS

Soapdodging by phone

A real celebrity chef

Being a renowned authority on a vast array of subjects, it is nevertheless quite probable that – if selected as a contestant for *Mastermind* – Welsh would opt for *Crossroads* as his specialist subject. That wonderfully crap soap opera, which peaked in the seventies, was favoured viewing for both of us and I turned several shades of green with envy on learning that he had somehow secured the autograph of Ronald Allen (i.e. David Hunter). This was lovingly pasted into his *Crossroads* scrapbook, along with photographs of stars such as Noele Gordon, a.k.a. Meg Mortimer, nee Richardson, and the lovely Jane Rossington. However, it wasn't until many years after the demise of this groundbreaking drama that I really came to appreciate his masterly knowledge of all things relating to King's Oak.

I had been at an all-night party in Livingston, when the talk turned (as it often does on such occasions) to Shite Soap Operas We Have Known and Loved. Of course, the motel saga was well to the fore. Another guest fancied himself as a bit of an authority and before long, we were drunkenly and childishly testing each other's powers of recall. But as I was at least twice as drunk as him, he had the advantage from the start.

"Who played Jill Harvey then?" I asked hopefully, remembering Irv's scrapbook.

"Easy, Jane Rossington," he declared. "What was the hippy gardener called?"

"Eh . . . Buzz," I gasped. "Who was the hairdresser who lived on the houseboat?"

"Vera. Name of the Salvation Army girl?"

"Jane. Who played Shooey McPhee?"

"Angus Lennie. Come on – you're not even testing me! Who played Paul Ross the chef, then?"

"Eh?"

"You heard!"

I had. And he had *me,* I realised. I could visualise the smarm-dripping smoothy no problem but I was fucked if I could recall his real name. Paul Ross, played by . . .???

My adversary was smiling triumphantly. "Food for thought there, I think!" he mocked as he got up to take a leak.

There was only one thing for it, I realised, as the door shut behind him. Desperate measures were called for. I hesitated for only a couple of seconds on considering the time and day of the week (5.30 a.m., Sunday) before diving for the telephone. I hastily dialled and waited with bated breath. After what seemed like an age, a grumpy and sleepy voice answered.

"Hallo?"

"Irvine! Who played Paul Ross in *Crossroads*?"

"Sandor Elès," came the immediate reply, followed by the phone banging down forcefully. I had only just managed to push the evidence away from me when my adversary returned.

"Well?" he demanded.

"Sandor Elès," I beamed back.

His face fell.

"You really know your stuff," he acknowledged in disappointment. "I thought I had you there."

It was possibly the greatest *Crossroads* moment of Welsh's career, at least until we saw the guy who played ruthless tycoon J. Henry Pollard put in a totally unexpected appearance in *Cry Freedom*. We rolled around the cinema, helpless with laughter. Had Dickie Attenborough lost his marbles or what??

15

STARFISH ON THE BEACH

"Waiter! There's a novelist in my lamb bhuna!"

In 1987, when I was reluctantly incarcerated in the Royal Mail sorting office in Brunswick Road, an early morning Saturday shift would finish at 11 a.m., which is at least a damned handy time of day to knock off, for obvious reasons. So one morning, I headed up to The Windsor to rendezvous with Irvine at that very hour. He was back living in Edinburgh and dying to meet a work colleague I'd told him about – an aggressively gay, campari-and-soda drinking, Freddie Mercury obsessed ex-squaddie, who had been attacked one morning on his rounds by a fierce . . . *owl*. Well, there was always a first time. No use in peeping fearfully over the garden gate in anticipation of Rover nipping your ankles when Hitch-cockian elements are swooping savagely out of the skies. But Big Ecky was on a back-shift, thus sadly missing out on the chance of featuring in a future Welsh novel. So it was just the two of us, as we slowly pub-crawled our way round to The Jailhouse for an afternoon gig.

By the time Roddy MacKenzie's Booze Brothers had lurched off the stage around 5 p.m., we had already imbibed a considerable quantity of alcohol. We staggered up Leith Street, hit the pubs in West Register Street and then poured ourselves into The Talisman in Waverley Station.

For some reason, this anonymous dump had always attracted us. Pubs in places of travel arrivals and departures are notoriously awful, where no one stays any longer than they have to, i.e. until it's time for their connection. At least, no one apart from us. On one occasion, when he'd been scheduled to travel to London on a noon train, I'd gone along to see him off and we'd popped into The Tally for "a quick one". After three, Irv decided to catch the 2 p.m. train. However, as he was halfway through a drink when 2 p.m. arrived, he opted to settle for the 4 p.m. train. . . . One thing led to another, and to another, and then another, and at midnight we were still sitting in exactly the same place. The barman was most impressed.

"I've never seen *anyone* drink so much in here in one day," he told us.

"We near London yet?" slurred Welsh hopefully. He went back to try again the following day.

This time we weren't quite so far gone – having been on the sauce for only about seven hours – but near as dammit. Irvine then badgered me out of the bar for some unknown reason and, still clutching half-pint tumblers and nips of whisky, we boarded a train. "Where are we going?" I demanded.

"Haymarket."

Well, that was OK then. I'd feared it might have been York, Grantham, London, Scarborough. . . . Why we were catching a train for a four-minute hop across Edinburgh was beyond me but I was in no state to ask difficult questions. That was brought home to me when the train suddenly lurched into motion, causing me to fall right across an elderly couple seated at a table. They jumped in alarm as a torrent of beer and whisky splashed into their laps.

"WATCH THAT MAN CLOSELY – HE'S A HEROIN PUSHER!!" shouted Irvine at the top of his voice to the whole carriage. Thank Christ it's a short trip, I thought, blanching as a hundred pairs of accusing eyes glared in my direction.

We tumbled off at Haymarket and tried manfully to ascend the steps leading to the exit. Rubber-legged, it was like trying to walk up a descending escalator. After several attempts, we managed to reach the top and clumsily barged through the swing doors.

"Tickets please!" shrilled an excitable voice from behind. In reply, Irvine tossed his glass over his shoulder Begbie-style and the voice ceased as if by magic. It was really only then that I realised how far gone we were, and in broad daylight too, which always seemed to make it worse. Too many sober people about. Even football casual types were drawing away from us as we were automatically sucked towards the magnetic force exercised by the secret machine in Ryrie's cellar.

As we fell in through the side door, I knew right away that if I had little chance of getting served, Irvine had absolutely none at all. A man of myriad talents but acting straight when out of his face had never been one of them. With this is mind, I made confused hand signals to indicate he should lurk in the shadows while I attended to a task roughly akin to climbing Mount Everest without oxygen. People were staring at us again, I thought irritably, as I forged ahead. Two of them looked familiar and I realised that Irvine was now half-propped up against their table, glassily staring at them. They appeared horrified and with little wonder . . .

Holy Christ! Now he was trying to kiss one of them! I stumbled into reverse gear with difficulty. As I made to grab my companion by the collar, I simultaneously attempted to focus on the two clearly agitated females, who by an astonishing coincidence closely resembled Irvine's mother and wife. By the time I'd refocused, I realised that this was not surprising, as they *were* his mother and wife. I sagged against the cigarette machine like a deflated space-hopper.

"It's our wedding anniversary," whispered Anne miserably.

"I'll get the drinks in," I gasped, retracing my steps hurriedly.

At the bar, things proceeded reasonably smoothly. I had to wait for service, giving me time to compose myself, calm down a bit and act a bit more sober. I saw that Burst Mattress-Heid was serving, which wasn't too bad. The head man was fairly tolerant as long as you didn't cross a certain line – when he promptly turned into a raving maniac and started calling 999. But "happily half-pissed" would be acceptable, I judged. So it seemed, as he approached, with a knowing smile smeared across his face.

"Two pints of heavy please, a Bacardi and coke and . . ."

I was rudely interrupted by a fearful crash from behind.

"GOODBYE TO YOU MY TRUSTED FRIEND . . ."

Oh no.

"WE'VE KNOWN EACH OTHER SINCE WE WERE NINE OR TEN . . ."

I still couldn't bring myself to look.

"TOGETHER WE CLIMBED HILLS AND TREES . . ."

I turned round slowly.

"SKINNED OUR HEARTS AND SKINNED OUR KNEES . . ."

Irvine was up on the table, surrounded by a sea of broken glass, I could see that much.

"GOODBYE TO . . ."

And goodbye it certainly was. Burst Mattress-Heid leapt into action swiftly and Welsh's rendition of the old Terry Jacks' tear-jerker never even made it as far as the first chorus. He was unceremoniously jerked off the table by mine host, who – perhaps regretting his leniency in not dialling 999 right away – issued three red cards on the spot instead.

"You, you and you – barred."

Still, if his mother had been receptive to the wisdom passed down by generation to generation within the Welsh family, she might have known what to expect. In her seventies, Irvine's granny visited a pub for the first and last time in her life, as her grandson's behaviour contributed to her being red-carded from The Foot-ballers' Arms in Easter Road.

Fifteen minutes later, the anniversary party was asked (politely this time) to vacate a nearby Chinese restaurant after Irv went to sleep in the curry – not an unusual occurrence maybe, but this time it wasn't even his own. "Too much wine and too much song," as Terry Jacks once observed. But, on this occasion, no joy, no fun and no seasons in the sun for the Mrs Welshes.

16

TENTACLES OF THE OCTOPUS

Plant pots

Squirling ink

The fanzine link

"I canny print this stuff – I really will get sued this time!"

The agitated speaker on the other end of the line was the then editor of *Hibs Monthly* football fanzine, who had just received some material from a person he knew to be a friend of mine. That person was known only by the strange pseudonym of "Octopus". (This name had been bestowed unwittingly on him by an outraged woman, who had slapped him hard, yelling "You! You've goat airms like a fuckin' octopus!") The eight-tentacled scribe had submitted a piece purporting to be the True Facts concerning a football club chairman, which Colin was understandably having cold feet about printing. The proud boast on the fanzine's mast-head declaring, "Sue us if you like – but we haven't any money!" had finally been put to the test.

I contacted the author of the article, who preferred to remain in the shadows of the 'zine world, never including his real name or address with any of his submissions.

"Colin says he can't print that stuff you sent him," I explained. "Too dodgy."

"But it's all true!" he yelled. "Every word of it! I have witnesses!"

"Doesn't matter. He's still not going to print it."

"Well – if he doesn't, *someone* will."

And so they did. That someone being publishers Jonathan Cape, as *Marabou Stork Nightmares* hit the bookstands many years hence, in 1995. There, in the chapter entitled 'The Pursuit of Truth', was the gross scene wherein three prostitutes urinate into plant pots, as a nasty capitalist masturbates in front of them.

To this day, those not cognizant of the fact that the novel is partly a cunning allegory about a failed football club take-over (i.e. most of the critics who originally reviewed it) may well still be asking – *Just who the hell is Lockhart Dawson???*

In the mid eighties, a strange, hitherto unknown publication could be observed up and down the country, circulating football stadia prior to kick-off. A magazine-type thingy of variable quality was being offered for sale, which at first glance might have been mistaken for "yir offishul programme!" This was, of course, the embryonic "fanzine", borrowing from the punk-ethos productions of the previous decade, which strove to give the real fans a chance to air their views in print. With club programmes generally promoting a bland, sycophantic and safe style of prose (in between the adverts), the emergence of the ubiquitous fanzine was a much-needed breath of fresh air.

Generally cheaper than yiroffishulprogramme, fanzines were by turn witty, provocative, childish, biased and controversial, but above all *genuine*, being put together for little profit by those with a real love of the game and their own particular club. I had been contributing to a selection of 'zines since late 1987 and it wasn't long before Welsh joined the ranks, submitting a series of very funny articles and skillfully drawn cartoons. The man's artistic qualities may have been overlooked since his emergence as a writer, but since a consistently good cartoonist is one thing that most liked-minded publications lack, Irv's talents were much appreciated by the various editors.

The self-styled "Octopus" first contributed to *The Hibees Glasgow Gossip* fanzine in August 1988 (Issue 10) with a four-frame cartoon strip entitled "Lexo", poking fun at the then Hibs Manager Alex Miller. By the next edition, this had extended to six frames and was a portent of things to come elsewhere. "Evil business person Wallet Mercenary and his faithful hound Diddy" made an appearance, with both cropping up later in a slightly different guise in *Marabou Stork Nightmares*. But by the time his moniker had evolved into "The Sinister Hibernian Octopus" in December of that year, the fanzine was on its last legs. Editor Dave Jackson moved away to London (where he was later instrumental in setting up *Hibees Here, Hibees There*) and the last issue appeared in January 1989.

By the late summer of that year, Irv had produced an excellent "Pseudo-Hun Bigot" (i.e. Hearts supporter who adopts Ibrox-esque militant Protestant tendencies) cartoon for *The Proclaimer*, as well as contributing an incisive analysis of the world of professional sports-writing, in the appropriately titled "Read All About (Sh)it". Mike Wilson's *The Proclaimer* was a sporadic publication, however, and before long we had both jumped ship in the direction of *Hibs Monthly*, the longest established Hibs fanzine. Later known as *Mass Hibsteria*, the original *Monthly* was founded by Colin Leslie and Stevie Burns when both were still at school and was a most professional job.

In Issue 24 (October 1989), Irvine weighed in with a new cartoon strip under his short-lived new alias of "Leith Lounge Lizard". This concerned the adventures of "Specky the Short-Sighted Jambo", the "smart, specky git with a solar-powered calculator", and interestingly enough, dealt with one of Specky's main hobbies, which just happened to be trainspotting.

A month later, he produced "Footy and the Beasts – Ugly Bastards of Scottish Football: An Appreciation". The beastly ball-players included ex-Hibs no-hoper "Benny" Brazil, Dave MacPherson and Brian "Roger" Whittaker of Hearts, David Dodds – "the plastic surgeon's nightmare" – then with Rangers and his team-mate of the time, Graeme Souness. I still cannot fathom Irv's assertion that Souey resembled Gail Tilsley from *Coronation Street* but the following outline of the man's appearance is, I think, hard to find fault with: "Take ET's chin, stick on a parrot's beak, a gay-scene clone moustache, top it off with a Benny Brazil haircut – and don't forget the goat's eyes!"

Well, quite. This edition also featured a finely-drawn cartoon depicting Hibs tough-tackling defender Gordon Hunter, who of course appeared with Yoko Ono in frankly alarming scenes of surrealistic cannibalism in *Trainspotting*.

Irvine was always quick to introduce new characters and although Specky continued to appear in either cartoon or columnar form, we were also treated to the exploits of other club's fans. Tam Porter – Motherwell Supporter – was the first of these and in Issue 27, a little fun was had at the expense of the, er, "style" of *The Sunday Post* Fun Section. "Jings! Crivvens! It's Donnie MacPhee From Bonnie Dundee!" announced the headline. (Linguistic students could also ponder the traditional cry of the fitba' ground salesman with his tray of goodies: "ERZIMAKAROON-BAURZNSPEERMINTCHUNEGUM!")

In a two-part "Hibs Pub Crawl" feature, Irvine extolled the virtues of The Cooper's Rest, thus: "The Cooper's retains its position as one of the most important institutions in Western culture. The neighbouring sister-bar The Cedar Lounge is a seething cauldron of romance and decadence, bringing to mind nothing less than the Berlin of the 1930s." In truth, it brought to mind nothing less than a vision of auld worthies with flat caps and their dugs on pension day, but what the hell.

He was less kindly to the other Leith howffs: "Fine ale, tasteful décor, warm friendly clientele bubbling over with sparkling wit and intellect. All are conspicuous by their absence at The Collie Dug. Given this, it would have to be a Jambo stronghold."

The Clan emerged as "the most marvellously disgusting pub in the galaxy", which, although undeniably true at the time, failed to do credit to the robust charm of the place. For years it had served as our meeting place prior to Hibs games and who could have failed to be impressed by some of the everyday sights therein? Live mouse catching, heroin dealing, go-go dancing, cankerous Alsatian dogs snarling, faded speedway stars reminiscing, the old tattooed barmaid glowering, the equally heavily tattooed and skin-grafted "Half-a-Poof", a fifty-five-year-old alcoholic Elvis Presley and Bruce Lee aficionado with coke-bottle specs kung fu kicking the walls . . .

The Boundary Bar, which featured in a post-party scene in *Trainspotting*, was dismissed as "not a place to be photographed if you're a fashion-conscious Hibby". Still, how many fashionable photographers are generally to be found kicking about Leith Walk at 5.06 a.m.?

The following season, the local cafes and restaurants came under equally merciless scrutiny in "The Hungry Hibby's Good Grub Guide". When working on the parks, the author had rejoiced in the nickname "Pig of Craigmount", in homage to his curry demolishing skills, so he was undoubtedly well qualified for this task. The categories included: "Italian, Chinese, Indian, Greasy Spoon and Chippy", with the following rating system:

★★★★★ *Pure Radge*

★★★★ *Barry*

★★★ *No' Bad*

★★ *Crap*

★ *Bring Wallace*

(The last referring to the supernaturally unpopular Heart of Midlothian FC chairman of the time.)

Under "Greasy Spoon", Irvine reported on a certain premises which better remain nameless as follows: (★) "Fat, peroxide, tattooed women struggling with prams, shopping and screaming shell-suited brats who hurl chips at each other compete for table space with hatchet-faced, stewed tea-guzzling, varicose-veined old crones in a bizarre ritual of death." For good measure, he also added that I occasionally dined there . . .

By Issue 36, the virginal Specky's chronic short-sightedness reached alarming proportions as he attempted to bag-off with Maggie Thatcher at a Tory fund-raising do, and a new cartoon appeared, satirising the "Heads You Win" photographs that would crop up in the local press at the time. (A fan in the crowd captured at random by the camera would be in line for some shoddy prize.) Irv's bogus competition boasted of "£75 worth of social security vouchers, exchangeable for the best quality second-hand merchandise at most second-hand shops in the Govan area." Beneath the picture containing a dozen or so horrendous looking characters, the caption ran: "Our circled man is described as stocky, unshaven, with a ruddy complexion, ginger sideboards, bushy eyebrows, and is sporting a 1970s style 'star' jersey, the type of which was popular in the era of 'Rollermania'." Part of the joke lay in the fact that *all* those featured possessed the same characteristics.

Targeted shortly afterwards was the traditional lifestyle as enjoyed by Scottish soccer "stars" of the time, or at least the tabloid versions of it. "Obese Jim Baxter's School of Soccer Excellence" featured Jimmy Sandison ("Sandy Jamieson" in *Marabou* speak) issuing report cards to younger players out on the town under the following categories:

Consuming Vast Quantities of Alcohol and Being Sick
Losing Large Sums of Money in the Bookmaker's
Chasing the Manto (i.e. The Mantovani, or Opposite Sex)
Getting Thrown Out of Tacky Italian Eating Houses
Swedging with Radges whilst Steamboats
Consuming Vast Quantities of Fried Food From Chip Shops
Standing Around in "Stylish" Nightclubs (i.e. With Watered Down Drinks, Mirrored Balls on the Ceiling and Chart 12 Inch Rap/Soul Singles).

Needless to say, all those assessed scored high marks in every category . . .

In March '91, "Hibs Pub Crawl" had reappeared, with a nostalgic portrayal of The Brunswick: "I was served there when I was given the short shrift in every pub, as an acne-stricken anti-social yob who blushed and farted every time a good looking woman came into the vicinity. It must have been all of last week."

That year's *Summer Special* saw an inspired Welsh cartoon front cover, depicting the discredited Hibs chairman and his chief executive as *Viz* comic's "Fat Slags", and a thoughtful (for once serious) inside article about the sense of bringing back the "Hands Off Hibs" campaign. The original movement had been set up to fight off a hostile bid from Lockhart Dawson type forces in 1990 and Irv was right to suggest a need for constant vigilance from the fans.

And elsewhere, while Specky paid a visit to "The Trouser Snake" Massage Parlour, I weighed in with the following article, concerning a "true-life" event:

Scene: Weedjieland

Date: The day Souness did a runner from Ibrox (during playtime, when teacher wisnae looking).

Man in street with microphone: "Excuse me, Sir, are you by any chance a Rangers supporter?"

Passer-by: "Eh? Uh . . . oh yes."

Man with microphone: "Good. Well you're on Radio Clyde – LIVE – and can you perhaps tell us what YOU think about Graeme Souness' departure from Rangers?"

Passer-by: "Best thing that's ever happened to them."

(Murmurs of disbelief and shock from Microphone Man, as interested Ibroxian types now gather round.)

Man with microphone: "Well . . . that's a different point of view . . ."

CARSPOTTING

Passer-by: (warming to his theme): Yes, it's true. He's RUINED the club. Rangers have always had a proud WHITE PROTESTANT SCOTTISH tradition, and what has he done but BASTARDISE this tradition by importing hordes of BLACKS, MERCENARY ENGLISHMEN . . . and CATHOLICS??"

(Mixed reaction from growing audience – cries of abuse, stunned silence, one loud cry of "Well said the big man! Needed to be said! Fucking well needed to be said," from the largest, most evil-looking bear in the group.)

Man with microphone (hurriedly): ". . . yes, well thank you for that comment, that will be all . . ."

(Passer-by strolls off casually whilst vicious verbal battle breaks out between White Supremacist Sons of William and their marginally more liberal contemporaries, with a good chance of blows eventually being exchanged all round.)

And now the point of this article . . .

Q: So who was this mysterious passer-by?

A: None other than the cleverly disguised *Hibs Monthly* correspondent Octopus, who just happened to be in Glasgow for the day, and felt obliged to put the cat amongst the pigeons in his usual time-honoured fashion . . .

The bogus bluenose was back on form in Issue 47, in the wake of Hibs' youth team's victory over their traditional adversaries. A cartoon showed a charity worker outside Tynecastle, rattling a can hopefully in the direction of the Hearts chairman:

"Mister Mercenary. Anything for the Sick Kids?"

"Yes. Several free transfers . . ."

By the time the following season was underway, Irvine was hard at work on his first novel and understandably, his contributions to the wacky world of fanzines began to dry up. Specky went out in a blaze of glory . . . or vomit, oral sex and smack injection on the

Merchiston Hearts bus to be exact, and in Issue 54, I advertised the imminent publication of *Trainspotting* under the headline "GEEBSY IN CRAZED CANNIBALISM HORROR!" (Geebsy being the nickname of the player gnawing bones in the book's "Yoko Ono dream sequence" section.)

Issue 58 in early 1994 saw *The Acid House* promoted in similar lurid fashion – "HIBS FAN STRUCK BY LIGHTNING IN PILTON WHILST UNDER THE INFLUENCE OF DRUGS SHOCK" I duly reported. Yes, loveable Hibs casual Coco Bryce (ya radge) had been well and truly frazzled (ya bass). His creator was now filthily rich and famous. As they say in all the crappest American teen horror flicks, "After that summer, things would never be the same again . . ."

FRANCIS BEGBIE V PATRICK BATEMAN

Psycho Analysis

Visiting the Man one day in his newly acquired Leith pad for the official "Prat of the Year" voting (in which we annually nominated the biggest eejit of the last twelve months from our circle of acquaintances), I found him thoughtfully pacing the floor and studying a sheaf of papers.

"Just something I've been working on for a while," he casually explained, indicating a monstrous mound of A4 sheets piled on a nearby desk. On the top page was printed the ominous word *Trainspotting*.

He then proceeded to read aloud from the sheaf in his hand, flinging each one over his shoulder in a style reminiscent of William Burroughs composing *Naked Lunch* in Tangier. And as Jack Kerouac had recoiled on perusing what he termed *Nude Supper* for the first time, I similarly blanched at the aural assault of Irvine's prose. Horrible stuff, indeed.

Beginners' instructions for concocting a vile literary stew — take the most unsavoury ingredients from Hubert Selby's *Last Exit to Brooklyn* and Celine's *Journey to the End of the Night*, sprinkle heavily with a strong dose of Urban Scots demotic, and marinate overnight in Bukowski. In fact, some of this was *so* extreme, it was edited out before the final draft was accepted for publication.

"Whaddya think?" demanded the author eagerly.

CARSPOTTING

At that point, I was let off the hook by his then wife Anne, who had looked up from the book she was reading.

"Irvine – that sounds *really* gross!"

Well, I was glad that at least someone was of similar mind. Still, as Anne was such a sweet-natured, sensitive soul, with a beguiling air of innocence about her even after years of being exposed to Welshian excess, I wasn't too surprised. And why, indeed, should any woman be subjected to such filth??

Just then I caught sight of the cover of the book she had lowered. It was *American Psycho*.

CLOCKING OFF

Trainspotting

A rude awakening

Identity crisis

Degradation in Dalry

When *Trainspotting* hit the bookshops in 1993 "like a stink-bomb from hell", as one critic deftly put it, its impact was instantaneous. I wasn't surprised. Irvine had employed me as a proofreader (the agreed fee was £20 – an astronomical sum for someone on the dole) and its impact on me was certainly that. I read it solidly over two days and was blown away by its power and black humour. There are very few books that leave you feeling you've gone fifteen rounds with Mike Tyson but this was undoubtedly one of them. It was immaterial that it had been written by a friend of mine – I felt much the same sense of awe as I had after reading Kerouac's *On the Road*, Steinbeck's *The Grapes of Wrath* or Tolkien's *The Lord of the Rings* for the first time.

I thought I'd better give him a bell. "Irv?"

"Aye . . . what do you reckon then?" he asked nervously.

"You're on a winner."

"Yeah?" He still sounded doubtful.

"Definitely. Mind you, I'm only saying that to get the twenty quid."

For me, the main power of *Trainspotting* was its unique approach to depicting the lifestyles of those for whom heroin use is a fact of life. William Burroughs had cast his cold clinical eye on the subject from his own experiences with the drug in *Junky* and there had been a plethora of "shock horror" type "confessional" books, but this was really the first to portray the junky "underclass" as real people living real lives. The only remotely comparable work I could think of was Hubert Selby Junior's classic, *Last Exit to Brooklyn*.

As with that grimly fractured narrative, the tone of *Trainspotting* never lets up and the dialogue between the characters is never less than wholly convincing. To portray the hilariously inarticulate Spud through his own voice when narrating cannot have been an easy trick to pull off – seeking to convey the thoughts, motives and aspirations of someone who hasn't got the vocabulary to do so for himself. In places, the steam-hammer rhythmic punch of the prose – bam-bam-fuckin'-BAM (take *that*, ya bam!) feels like nothing less than a full-on frontal assault on the reader. Stunningly effective and compelling. Whether or not *Trainspotting* stands the test of time overall, it's probably still too early to say, but its influence continues to resonate from what now seems like a lost time zone from another planet. But an era-defining novel? Most definitely.

So, Irvine's career (if that's indeed what it was) had gone instantly stratospheric. *Trainspotting* iconography was seemingly everywhere for a while and everyone was wanting a piece of it. I used to drink in Mathers at the West End at the time and Irv would occasionally join me. He soon had to stop, however. Guaranteed he would be recognised and the person would yell, "Just stay there for a minute!" before dashing along to Waterstone's on Princes Street for a copy of the book. So Irvine would have another pint and wait patiently for his latest admirer to return and request for an autograph to be scrawled on the hallowed tome.

"I can't go on like this!" he wailed. "I really like meeting people who appreciate it and am always happy to talk to them, but at this rate I'll *never* get out of the pub!"

"No change there, then," I remarked.

He freely admitted that had this whole circus erupted when he was younger, the financial rewards would probably not have been entirely conducive to his continuing good health. Being thrust suddenly in the spotlight's glare is not always a good thing – particularly if it happens to someone with all the self-restraint of Keith Richards let loose in a poppy field.

As the launch date for his second book started to loom on the distant horizon, I asked him if there had ever come a point when he'd felt that the whole hoopla had just grown to unreal dimensions. We were sitting in the sanctuary of the Film House Café Bar, just the two of us, as he'd felt a need for some respite from all the madness. He paused thoughtfully before answering.

"I think it must have been in New York," he finally said "I mean, I'd only got to meet my all-time rock idol Iggy Pop – I gave him a Hibs strip to wear on stage. But I was so tongue-tied I could hardly speak. He told me to call him Jim but I was so nervous I kept mixing it up with Iggy, so it just came out all wrong. Then he finally said, 'Er-vine, man! Don't worry – just call me Jiggy! Now come on, we're gonna go meet Jim-Jam and Marianne!'"

"Jim-Jam and Marianne?" I echoed.

"Yeah, that's what I said! So we pitched up at this sleazy club, where we came across Jim Jarmusch the film director and Marianne Faithfull – who'd had a few too many. Next thing I know, I'm sitting there with a 1960s goddess practically in my lap, shooting the breeze with Jim-Jam, while Iggy's at the bar getting the round in! 'Whaddya want to drink Er-vine?' he's shouting, while one of his own records comes on the jukebox." Irvine put down his glass, exhaled a deep breath and looked me in the eye. "That," he said exhaustedly, "was when it all became just a bit *too* unreal . . ."

Fast-forward a few months into 1994 . . .

"Brr brr! Brr brr! Brr brr!" The terrible noise gradually permeated through the black sludge in my semi-comatose brain and one limp hand groped for the light switch. Once the latter had been activated, I was aghast to discover that it wasn't even 10 a.m.

yet – practically the crack of dawn. I placed the receiver to my ear, croaked out a greeting and recoiled in alarm as a bright, cheerful, upper-class English female responded instantly. I recoiled even further when she then sought to clarify my identity.

I debated inwardly for a moment. Admitting to being who she thought I was might throw up an endless series of complications, which I was particularly ill-equipped to deal with at the time. I had only recently denied that I was such a person to an unidentified caller in the nick of time, as she then revealed herself to be a representative of Sheriff's officers. As the latter were – indeed probably still are – pursuing me for a ridiculous sum of money, I couldn't be too careful. But in my rudely awakened state, I couldn't think of an alternative. So I agreed, guardedly, that I was that man.

"I believe that you are proofreading Irvine Welsh's latest book for us?" continued the lady in a business-like voice, going on to identify herself as an employee of Jonathan Cape publishing house. Well, that was a relief at any rate. I looked vaguely around the room until my eye came to rest on a large beer-splattered manuscript. Then I recalled the same object being unceremoniously shoved into my hands by Welsh in Ryrie's, some twelve hours previously. It must be true then.

"Yes," I admitted finally.

"I take it that Mr Welsh explained all the conditions and requirements to you?"

This lassie was undoubtedly taking a lot for granted.

"Uh . . . no."

So she went on to explain them instead. Twenty minutes later, I put the phone down exhaustedly and went back to sleep. When I awoke, I had of course forgotten virtually all that she'd told me – apart from the part concerning payment.

After breakfast (burnt toast and lager), I sat down at the kitchen table with *The Acid House* in front of me. Irvine's phone number was also at hand, in case of any unforeseen difficulties with the contents. I seemed to recall him reassuring me that there wouldn't be, round about the eighth pint the previous evening. The main things to watch out for were much the same as when I'd cast my beady eyes over *Trainspotting* for the first time, namely the rules regarding spelling. As part of the main text, words should be spelt as normal, whereas when radges were speaking (more or less incessantly as it turned out, with the welcome exception of that reticent lad Ronnie in *A Smart Cunt*) they should be spelt phonetically. Fairly straightforward then, once you got used to it.

The first frown creased my brow during "Stoke Newington Blues", wherein I instantly recognised the depiction of the police cells, containing "piss-heads, petty criminals and cannabis dealers". Myself and the author came under the first category during our brief stay there, certainly. (The one-eared transvestite mentioned in this story was transported for literary reasons from another police station where Irvine had previously been detained.) Bad memories . . .

As I proceeded, I also instantly recognised the narrator of "A Soft Touch", a thinly-disguised version of a supreme idiot who is still strutting the streets of Edinburgh today, and Robert K. Laird, whose brief sexual history was still longer on the printed page than in real life.

I was fast realising that *The Acid House* contained more genuinely "real" characters than its illustrious predecessor, when I was pulled up sharply by the distinctly surreal title of the story "Wayne Foster". I knew right away that honouring a Heart of Midlothian player in this way would lead to trouble, and so it proved. The pain of witnessing vital goals he subsequently put away against Hibs could well have been avoided, if Welsh hadn't tempted fate by lauding him in such a fashion. "Fast as fuck", indeed.

However, the text posed no real problems from a proofreading point of view (at this stage, the eyeball-frazzling acid trip lettering in the title story had yet to be added) and all was going swimmingly as I finished the short stories and started the novella.

Irvine had already alluded to his past employment on the Park Patrol in Renton's guise in *Trainspotting*, but here "Brian" was a bit more forthcoming about mischief-making down Inverleith way. (In reality, however, it was irresponsible dog owners rather than prepubescent schoolgirls who had most to fear from the parkie's acidic tongue in Welsh's heyday.)

It wasn't until I'd mentally pub-crawled my way through one of the many booze-soaked segments that I finally ground to a halt. Some of Edinburgh's finest watering holes had been rightly name-checked. Ryrie's, Sandy Bell's, The Spider's Web (known popularly as The Arachnaphobic Entanglement by local wits) but . . . what was this shit??? I reached for the telephone and dialled, one eye still on the text.

"Irv?"

"Yeah."

"Just where the fuck is the so-called Gorgie/Dalry Oyster Bar??"

The sound of the manic Welsh cackle issued from the other end.

"Do you mean the West End Oyster Bar?" I persisted hopefully.

"No."

"Well then?"

"Well, I just made it up. It's roughly where The Clock Inn is, I reckon."

I clapped my hands over my ears at once. "Don't mention The Clock!" I screamed and slammed the receiver down.

My hand trembled slightly as I reached unsteadily for the flat lager. Then a mental picture of my last experience in the concrete bunker from hell swam into focus and I dived for the sink, gagging uncontrollably . . .

Some years before, Irvine and myself had been enjoying an early evening drink, sitting opposite an old guy who had fallen asleep

CLOCKING OFF

(this was positively encouraged at the time, as it afforded local hoods the opportunity to pick your pockets with the minimum of fuss). He was soon joined in the Land of Nod by a wee skinhead who had collapsed next to him totally out of the box, using the old boy's shoulder as a pillow as he passed out. It was not long before a stream of multi-coloured vomit issued from the wee ned's open mouth, splattering into his elder's lap. Another spectacular eruption followed, before his head slipped back against the wall. For an encore, his last picturesque fountain caught the victim from his rear blind side just above the collar, whereupon he was suddenly and brutally seized by bar persons and flung into the street. A clear case of the "Three Spews and You're Out" policy at work.

We watched with interest as the diced carrot-encrusted victim finally awoke, regarding his waist area with no little horror. He slunk out embarrassed, no doubt under the impression that he'd been sick over himself. But what would happen when he undressed later that night, we wondered in morbid curiosity? Surely the following conundrum would puzzle and perplex him for years to come – namely: "HOW THE FUCK DID I MANAGE TO PUKE DOWN THE BACK OF MY OWN NECK???"

19

THE REAL BEGBIE

Frank revelations

A man called Motherwell

Cold, cold steel

"Two Francis Begbies, there's only two Francis Begbies . . ."

It could be fairly said that one of Scottish literature's most effervescent psychopaths was based mainly on two people – 1) a Glaswegian nutter Welsh had the misfortune to flat-share with in London once, and 2) an Edinburgh nutter who succeeded in drinking himself to death in his mid-thirties some years back.

The first psycho's dislike of "Embra bastards" (that is, folk native to the capital city of Scotland) was so intense that Irvine never plucked up the courage to own up to his Edinburgh roots. Observing the alarming effect that stating he was "from the east" had on Psycho No. 1, he hastily reinvented himself as a denizen of the fine city of Motherwell (which was at least east of Glasgow). This mollified his flatmate to some extent, who then resorted to using "Motherwell" as a derogatory nickname for Irv, causing the latter to realise that claiming Lanarkshire citizenship perhaps hadn't been such a good idea after all. However, he managed to affect a sneaky revenge for those months of living on his nerves before vacating the property and returning north of the border. He cunningly scratched Psycho No. 1's prized collection of mint condition Sensational Alex Harvey Band LPs in strategic places, a near sacrilegious act, which would become evident only when the owner attempted to sing along with the catchy choruses after returning home drunk of an evening.

CARSPOTTING

But although *Trainspotting* Begbie resembled this gentleman to some degree, it was Psycho No. 2 who provided most of young Franco's quirky characteristics and mannerisms. For example, the pub brawl scene in "The Glass" erupted more or less as described on the printed page, kicked off by Psycho No. 2 casually chucking a pint tumbler over his shoulder and then ruthlessly interrogating innocent bystanders to find out who'd glassed the victim. This occurred in the old Cottar's Howff bar in Rose Street, which has now been incorporated into Milne's on the corner of Hanover Street.

Sharpened knitting needles were indeed part of No. 2's armoury, with the real life Begbie testing their flesh-piercing potential by ramming them into an old mattress, which was propped up against the wall at the foot of his garden for this purpose. "The discipline ay the baseball bat" also featured in his everyday existence, as did "the cold, cold steel pressed against the naked skin". Not long after trying (and failing) to gas his hated younger brother, his marriage broke up and the Real Begbie predictably plunged headlong down the slippery slope. He ended up as a homeless wino, moving finally to a doss-house down in Leith. Amusingly enough, Irvine was also resident in the old port area at that point and had to take evasive action on numerous occasions. In the evening, he used to see Psycho No. 2 temporarily burying his stash of alcohol with the aid of a trowel in Leith Links, as it was forbidden to take it into the hostel. By this stage of his deterioration, he probably wouldn't have recognized Irvine (a good friend of his brother's) anyway but Welshy was taking no chances. He never even had the courage to dig up the buried bevvy after nightfall.

The Real Begbie was aged thirty-six when he died in hospital of liver cirrhosis, still howling defiantly at the world he hated. Irvine attended the funeral out of respect for his family, later employing some of the clichéd responses to untimely death in his account of Billy Renton's demise in *Trainspotting*.

THE REAL BEGBIE

When I spoke to Robert Carlyle at the film premiere (oh! how's that for name-dropping??), he said that he was initially apprehensive about taking on the role, as the character "seemed to literally burst out of every page" on which he made an appearance. Of course, he went on to play the part brilliantly, all the more convincingly as the role model wasn't your archetypal "screen heavy" in size but closer to the actor's own build. Robert couldn't have possibly known how near to the real thing he came in his portrayal.

As for the Real Thing – it would be stretching the truth to say that he was mourned by many, but his early demise certainly made a few people sit up and take stock of their own situation. In fact, he would be only the first in a long line of acquaintances who would kick the bucket in their late thirties or early forties, mainly as a result of leading crazy, out of control lives. Perhaps it was time for some of us to wise up?

20

ZORBA ONCE AGAIN

In Brendan Behan's footsteps, we danced up and down the street

Wise up? Who the fuck was I kidding? But perhaps this break from the local madness would do me some good, I thought, as the ferry pulled away from Stranraer on its way to Belfast. From there, it was a hopefully relaxing train ride to the Republic's capital and a much-needed chill-out. Perhaps my vague malaise was something to do with the company I was keeping? Ostensibly, I was there to hook up with a bunch of fellow regulars from The Roseburn who were flying over for a weekend at the races. However, Irvine had indicated that he also would be in the Fair City around this time, so doubtless we would hook up at some point. At this stage of the game, he was maintaining properties in both Edinburgh and London, but increasingly drawn to making a move to Dublin. House-hunting was possibly on the cards.

It was 1996 and *Ecstasy* had just been published, to less than ecstatic acclaim from the reviewers. Still, it shifted 50,000 copies in the first week of sales. He'd been kind enough to dedicate it to myself, so I sycophantically proclaimed it another rip-snorting classic. Or the page with my name on it at least.

Lost in reverie, I was startled by the Ian Paisley-esque accent barking over the Tannoy, announcing our imminent arrival point. Belfast! I shuddered as I recalled Irvine launching into an impromptu karaoke version of that Boney M "classic" in some hell-hole boozer, as a tribe of heavy metal aficionados at the next table were clearly contemplating beating him to a bloody pulp.

There was no doubt about it, I thought resignedly, that the worst person – bar none – to encounter when one is stone cold sober and the other is out of his box, is Welsh. For a kick off, most people are actually quite predictable in their behaviour when the bevvy starts to take its toll. You can usually tell which ones will sing, which will fall asleep, which will become maudlin, which will want to fight, and so on. The worst thing about Welsh drunkenness is its very unpredictability. You can never file it away neatly in the box marked "Talking Shite", "Winding Up Jambos" or whatever, because it's guaranteed to manifest itself in some ugly alternative format somewhere else down the line. Such were my ruminations as the door of McDaid's in Harry Street, Dublin, was viciously booted open to admit Irvine – in the "Incoherent Singing" phase, for the time being. I knew it was a bad sign when I saw that he had Anne gripped in the customary stranglehold, one arm folded tightly across her throat. This signified major inebriation.

However, as McDaid's had previously enjoyed infamy as a centre for Dublin bohemia in the fifties and sixties, they were a good deal more tolerant of such behaviour than most establishments back home. After all, Flann O'Brien, Patrick Kavanagh and Brendan Behan had all drank and fought here in their heyday, the latter supposedly painting the toilets for a "pint of plain" on one occasion. The famous old pub was very busy too, which helped to drown out the racket emanating from the arseholed author. Over the next three hours, I made out only one coherent statement, which fell from his lips after some twittery English woman recognised him.

"I just *love* your books – don't you remember, I met you at that reading in London last year?" she yipped excitedly.

"Fuck off you middle-class bitch," retorted Welsh, slightly pithily.

I tried to swiftly clamp my hand over his mouth (which I had many years' practice at) but it was too late. Possibly the background noise obscured his reply but she caught the general drift. Don't fuck with temperamental Jock writers, especially when they're steaming.

It would be unfair, however, to suggest that this alarmingly candid behaviour was typical. In fact, he was utterly contrite and remorseful when reminded of it later. Irv was usually incredibly patient when encountering fans, even when they got right in his face as this one had done. Normally, he was never less than appreciative of their interest in his work and genuinely liked meeting them.

I learned subsequently that around this time, he had acquired one of those unwelcome endorsements of celebrity status – a totally deranged and possibly dangerous stalker. Understandably stressed out over the situation, and particularly so when in his wife's company, he had initially thought that this was she. But it wasn't. So, if you're reading this, whoever you are, he would just like to say a belated "sorry!"

The following afternoon, I sat in O'Donoghue's, futilely waiting for the silver-tongued charmer to show. I'd done a runner from McDaid's about 10 p.m. the previous evening, when he'd reached the Oblivious-to-the-World, Glass-Dropping stage, but I knew Anne would remind him of this rendezvous. Still, one hour had passed and there was no sign. I knew that he'd been installed on the publisher's tab at one of the top hotels, which was just along the road. So, after polishing off another pint of Guinness, I rather reluctantly left the convivial atmosphere behind and headed across Merrion Row.

As a scruffy down-at-heel sort of person, I never felt very comfortable entering such palatial places, particularly in search of Welsh. Who knew what outrage he may have committed on returning from McDaid's? If you're shelling out several hundred quid per night for the privilege of staying in a top-notch gaffe, the last thing you want is some drunken Scottish oaf with an Iggy Pop fixation indulging in behaviour in the next room that would put Keith Moon to shame. With this in mind, I approached the desk hesitantly.

"Yes, sir?" said a grave-looking, immaculately dressed, elderly desk clerk.

I pricked up my ears for any sarcastic inflexion on the "sir" but failed to detect one.

"Eh . . . I was meant to meet up with a friend who is staying here and he hasn't turned up. Could you possibly page his room?"

"The name, sir?"

"Mr Irvine Welsh," I admitted, watching closely for any reaction. I thought I espied a brief shudder but it might have just been my imagination.

"One moment, sir."

His gnarled hand reached out for the telephone and after consulting the register, he dialled a number. On establishing contact, he passed the receiver across.

"Irv?"

"Uh . . ."

"Irvine, is that you?"

"Eh . . . uh . . ."

Oh Christ, the clerk was giving me the suspicious eye, I was sure of it.

"Irvine!"

"Aye!"

"It's me. I thought you were coming down to O'Donoghue's for three o'clock?"

"Uh . . . what time is it now?"

"Quarter past four."

"Are you *sure*?"

"Yes."

"Oh . . . I've just woken up . . . I feel like shite . . . Oh no! OH FUCK! I DON'T BELIEVE IT! Oh fuckin hell . . ."

The voice trailed off despairingly.

"Irv? What is it?"

He croaked out a reply, which I initially misinterpreted as, "I've been horrible." Well, that was certainly true.

"You were horrible last night all right."

"No, no! I've been *ZORBA*!"

"You've been what?"

"Zorba, I've been Zorba the Greek . . . all over the fuckin' Burke and Hare!"

As fans of his punchy prose will be aware, the man just loves to indulge in a spot of gratuitous rhyming slang when the mood takes him (especially when he's made it up himself, as opposed to borrowing from the official Cockney form). Therefore, I swiftly deduced the cause of his distress – namely, that he'd been seek, on the flair.

"Is everything alright sir?" said a voice at my elbow.

"Eh? Oh aye, fine, thank you," I lied.

I tried to ignore his frowning visage as I tersely conveyed to the vomitee that he should move his arse in the direction of O'Donoghue's ASAP and replaced the receiver. The nosey old goat was still staring at me questioningly.

"Do *not* disturb," I advised, with a firm shake of the head. "And I don't think Mr Welsh will be requiring dinner."

About twenty minutes later, he floated into the boozer looking somewhat fragile and complaining of vertigo.

"Eh??"

"Well . . . I had to come out down the fire escape. I was too embarrassed to walk through reception."

I didn't even bother to ask what he'd been up to the night before.

Somehow we managed to secure two stools at what is surely one of the busiest bars on the entire island and tried to relax to the sounds of about a dozen folkies all playing different instruments, and quite possibly different tunes too. Around the fourth pint mark, we had been joined by the nice man from the publishers. He was urging Irvine to attend a short function that evening, with little sign of success.

"There'll be some important people there. Look, it's only for about half an hour, Irvine. I'll have a car pick you up at your hotel about eight o'clock."

"Uh-huh," he agreed unenthusiastically.

It transpired that he was actually on an official book–signing and promotional tour of the Emerald Isle, and was therefore effectively "at work".

"It's fair enough, I suppose," he acknowledged, swallowing a huge mouthful of the black stuff. "After all, they fly me first class all over the world, put me up in the best hotels, pay for all the extras, so I suppose the least I can do is put in the odd promo appearance."

"But?"

"But I feel like acting the spoilt brat for once!"

By the time 8 p.m. arrived, both of us had forgotten all about the pressing demands of the outside world. Until a worried figure hove into view . . .

"Oh no!" it gasped.

Irvine looked up glassily.

"I take it you're not going then?" enquired his long–suffering editor.

"Going? Going where??"

After Robin departed, I felt a pang of sympathy for anyone who had the misfortune to be landed with the responsibility of cajoling a petulant author around the place.

"He looked a bit . . ." observed Irv vaguely, searching for the appropriate word.

". . . Zorba?"

ZORBA ONCE AGAIN

"Yeah, that's it. A bit Zorba."

The following morning, Irvine and Anne flew first class to Heathrow Airport. I caught the Arnold Layne north, jumped the Tom and Jerry to Stranraer, took an ugly pus to Ayr, and then double-stitched a Jonathan Swift off a passing Mars Bar as far as Glasgow. What a Joe Strummer, man.

21

ON THE JEWEL CARRIAGEWAY

Red Bullshit

The wrong trousers

Liquid lesbians in Leith

So as the years rolled by and his books continued to sell by the truckload, the financial rewards ensured that Irv no longer needed to keep jazzing about up and down the country (and indeed to Amsterdam) to flee for pastures new when he so desired. He could now simply buy houses all over the fucking shop and live in whichever one suited him best at the time. His latest purchase was at the east end of Edinburgh's New Town, ideally suited for nights out at local literary salons such as The Phoenix and The Cask and Barrel.

"Well," I thought, as the taxi sped east across the city to the seldom-used Welsh pad, "at least you never have to worry about the fare when socialising with best-selling authors." The cab pulled up sharply at the kerb and the driver turned round expectantly. Welsh, blanching visibly at the monetary total displayed on the meter, made a great show of hunting around in his pockets. He finally extracted a grubby fiver and a two-pound coin and handed them over.

"Could I have a receipt, please?"

Oh no, indeed. Their long-suffering publishers have to worry about it instead.

The front door creaked open, revealing a gloomy interior. As the occupant hadn't been here in ages, the place had an eerie, empty feel to it – as if we were trespassing in a mausoleum. I conveyed this sense of unease to my companion, who snorted derisively.

"If you think this is spooky, you want to drop in upstairs sometime."

Not long after he'd moved in, the older couple there had hospitably invited him up for a drink. And not long after that, they received another visitor, in the shape of a deeply disturbed schizophrenic knifeman. He frenziedly attacked them both, killing one and seriously injuring the other.

"I'll be ten minutes, tops," he said, disappearing into the bedroom to get changed. "Pour us a drink."

I proceeded to open a multitude of kitchen cupboards at random, peering within.

"Unless you're up for a cheeky wee cobweb cocktail, we're out of luck."

"There's a bottle of fucking gin there somewhere. Keep looking!" Eventually, I located the said article, pulled it down and looked at it stupidly.

"Now what?"

"Oh Jesus! There should be an old can of Red Bull kicking about in the fridge I think."

I found that as well. "Old" was the operative word. I scanned in vain for a "use by" date but it had probably rusted over.

"You actually want me to mix them together?"

"Do we have a choice?"

I had already chucked one down my neck when Welsh emerged re-suited and booted.

"What's it like?"

"GR . . . AA . . . RR . . . AARH . . ."

I could feel the raging firestorm burn past my throat and start to ooze like molten lava down my gullet.

"Eh?"

ON THE JEWEL CARRIAGEWAY

"UUGH . . . YEAARGHHH!"

"That good, huh?"

I put the glass down shakily. Irvine was eagerly pouring himself a large shot.

"I can honestly say that's one of the most horrible drinks I've ever consumed."

I looked on in interest as his face galvanised in an expression of unpleasant shock.

"Fucking horrible," he agreed in a strangled croak.

I refilled my glass.

"It'll probably taste better after a few," I said pseudo-optimistically but fooling no one, least of all myself. "Congratulations on inventing a brand new pre-dinner aperitif. So what are you going to call it?"

An involuntary spasm jackknifed through the Welsh frame as his second one hit home. He looked thoughtful.

"Mm . . . let me see. Gin . . . gin and Red Bull . . . something that sounds like a mixture of the two. How about 'jewel'?"

"Jewel . . . or joule?"

"Uh?"

"Well, I dunno about you but it certainly feels like someone's just zapped a fucking electrical charge straight down my neck."

"Or 'duel' even? It's a mighty combative concoction all right."

We swallowed several more glasses and then headed out to hail a taxi, as I'd arranged to meet up with some workmates in Leith. Welsh refused point-blank to entertain the idea of public transport or – horror of horrors – *walking*. Then again, that might have proved problematic after the last cocktail hour or so.

The cab stopped on Leith Walk and the driver shut off the meter. "Five pounds, please."

Welsh's countenance indicated that he was suffering from a sudden severe case of constipation.

"Can you get this? I'm a bit short."

"Yeah, I couldn't help noticing you put the wrong trousers on back at the house, when you got changed."

"How do you mean, chief?"

"I mean, you only went and put on the pair without the fucking wallet in the pocket."

I paid off the driver huffily and we decamped at the doors of the appropriately named Windsor. Like the matriarch of the famous family, it now appeared that Welsh did not deign to carry common-as-muck cash about on his regal personage.

We started on the pints but it was impossible to shift the horrible metallic taste from our tongues. After a while, we were joined by two strident lesbians, whom His Majesty seemed to know vaguely from somewhere. Enthusiastic party-animals, they were celebrating a birthday.

"Whose?" I asked, looking from one to the other.

"k.d. lang's."

"My treat, then," announced Welsh, miraculously unearthing a stash of money concealed about his body.

"Four jewels," he informed the barman.

"*Eh??*"

"Four joules," I corrected. "You know – gin and Red Bulls."

"Oh, *joules*," he replied, in a brilliant display of mock recognition. "Coming right up!"

They certainly will be later on, I thought.

By the time I'd stumbled down to the foot of the Walk, the change in my demeanour must have been obvious. My workmates regarded me with no little alarm.

"Duals," I tried to explain, my swollen metallic tongue flapping drily in my sandpaper mouth like a dying fish.

"The concept of Duality. You know . . . the balance between Good and Evil, Jekyll and Hyde . . . Hibs and Hearts, Rodgers and Hammerstein . . ."

★

ON THE JEWEL CARRIAGEWAY

Next morning, the real duality of the after effects became crystal clear. The properties of each drink had contributed to this in their own unique way, so it could be said – at a push – that there was a definite down-side but happily also an up-side . . . of sorts. Namely, I felt suicidally depressed but for once, actually had enough fucking mis-wired energy crackling through my diseased body to follow through. That was surely the *real* jewel in the crown.

I phoned Welsh, to find him in a similarly pensive sorry-for-himself state.

"What the fuck did you start us off drinking that shite for?" he yelled. "Are you trying to kill me?!"

"It was your fucking idea in the first place!" I howled back, suitably outraged. "Don't blame me. That's just typical, it's like that time you went insane on V2 cider and accused your poor mother of trying to poison the entire Hibs team before the 1985 League Cup Final."

"I still think she had a hand in it," he muttered half-heartedly but I could sense his spirit was broken. "How are you feeling?"

"Terrible,' I reassured him. "I may have subliminally been trying to kill you but now I just feel like killing myself."

"Yeah?" he said, suddenly sounding more cheerful.

"Oh aye. But I daresay I'll get over it. We've been down, down, deeper and down before this 'n' bounced back, old buddy."

"We sure have."

"Do you realise how long it's been that we've been acting like arseholes united?"

"Mmm . . . we first met in that fucking horrible Civil Service job back in, what, '75 or '76? Well over thirty years then."

"Yeah. But we kinda knew each other vaguely before even that, remember? Travelling to the Hibs away games on the notorious Excursion buses run by Eastern Scottish . . ."

"Christ, aye. The Borstal on wheels. You were pals with Kenny

Soper, who was a mate of my pal John Till. And that was that. Must've been around '71 or '72."

"Long time ago."

"Aye."

Had the brain-addling and depressive properties in last night's hooch contributed to this "nostalgia ain't what it used to be" air of bittersweet reminiscing I wondered? There was silence at the other end.

"Irv . . ."

"Uh-huh?"

"I was just reading in the paper here that some dodgy entrepreneur is thinking of marketing gin and Red Bull cocktails for the Dutch market."

"Oh aye?"

"Yeah. You know what he's going to call it, don't you?"

"What?"

"Jewels Holland, of course."

"OH FUCK OFF!"

And on that poignant note, the line went dead.

EXTRAS:
DIRECT FROM THE
PRINTED PAGE

22

SCARY GEEZERS, EVERY ONE . . .

Best Irvine Welsh radges (originally published in *The Scotsman*, February 2008)

1. **FRANCIS BEGBIE** (*Trainspotting* and *Porno*)

An enthusiastic advocate of "the discipline ay the basebaw bat", young Frank's penchant for bullying, petty crime, constant swearing, mindless violence in general and – shockingly – pinching a reserved seat on a train, qualifies him as a classic Welshian character. "Beggars" finally gets his comeuppance of sorts at the end of *Porno*, as an innocent motorist succeeds where many other adversaries have failed.

2. **BRUCE ROBERTSON** (*Filth*)

Lothian and Borders' most corrupt cop is on a downward spiral, fuelled by self-loathing, cocaine binges and bad heavy metal. He cruises the mean streets of Edinburgh in frenzied pursuit of his own pleasure, increasingly irritated as police work intrudes. The murder victim is black, so of no real consequence, but Robertson is no mere racist, he hates everyone.

3. **DANNY SKINNER** (*The Bedroom Secrets of the Master-Chefs*)

The environmental health officer and raging alcoholic Lothario has little time for the detested master-chefs, but even less for his work colleagues. Soon, the hapless Brian Kibby is the unwitting focus for all Skinner's pent-up fury at the state of the world. In a series of escalating, blackly comic vignettes, his persecution of Kibby reaches unparalleled heights, before he too is the victim of an unexpected payback.

4. **LARRY** (*The Acid House*)

A man so radge he is not even credited with a surname, the protagonist sizes up his gormless neighbour as a real "soft touch". He steals his bevvy, his wife, even his electricity. Larry's nutter credentials are validated by the fact that the dreaded Doyles – the scheme's radgest family – deem him worthy of grudging respect.

5. **JOHN STRANG** (*Marabou Stork Nightmares*)

A role model for grumpy old men everywhere, the raving rightwing reactionary is patriarch of Muirhouse's most dysfunctional family. Often seen patrolling the scheme in his brown fur coat (concealing a shotgun with which he randomly threatens to shoot people), he is not amused when a joker paints an "e" at the end of his surname on the front-door nameplate.

★ Fascinating trivia fact: The inspiration for Mr Begbie's christian name came to Irvine as he peeped fearfully through his fingers at the screen in the darkened cinema. In homage to a fellow raving psychopath, "Beggars" is named after Dennis Hopper's character in *Blue Velvet* – the homicidal Frank Booth.

23

THE DIRTY DOZEN . . .

Top sporting moments from Irvine Welsh's first three books (originally published in *Mass Hibsteria* magazine, March 1996)

1. "The whole town was decked in green and white, songs were spilling out of every bar. It was a Hibbie's fantasy, not a Jambo in sight: they were still all skulking indoors contemplating thirty years without a trophy on the shelf."

The aftermath of the Hibs' 1991 Skol Cup semi-final win over Rangers as recounted by Roy Strang. (*Marabou Stork Nightmares*)

2. When unexpectedly having his "first shag in ages", Mark Renton desperately tries to forestall premature ejaculation by visualising himself committing anal intercourse with Hearts' chairman Wallace Mercer. (*Trainspotting*)

3. "Mickey Weir gets more protection from Syme at Ibrox than I ever did from that auld cunt." – junkie talking about his granny in *The Acid House*

4. Brian achieves orgasms while watching the football results on telly –
Aberdeen 6 (six), Heart of Midlothian 2.
Hibernian 3, St Johnstone 1.
(*The Acid House*)

5. Mickey Weir is referred to as "a wee honey" by Sick Boy. (*Trainspotting*)

6. Spud is so spaced out he imagines Gordon Durie is still playing for Hibs six years after his transfer to Chelsea. (*Trainspotting*)

7. Pat Stanton "with his '70s sideboards" frowns down disapprovingly from a wall poster as Renton endures agonising heroin withdrawal. (*Trainspotting*)

8. Unpopular football club chairman Lockhart Dawson performs perverted acts with prostitutes and plant-pots. (*Marabou Stork Nightmares*)

9. "I'd rather see my sister in a brothel than ma brother in a Hearts' scarf." – Sick Boy (*Trainspotting*)

10. Two eminent University professors knock seven types of shite out of each other before a baying mob of Rangers fans prior to an Old Firm game. (*The Acid House*)

11. The mysterious *Boys' Own*-type soccer hero referred to as Sandy Jamieson is finally revealed as being none other than Airdrie and ex-Hearts superstar Jimmy Sandison. (*Marabou Stork Nightmares*)

12. "Big time soccer violence in Scotland had always been about really thick Weedjies who never went to church knocking fuck out of each other to establish who had the best brand of Christianity." – Roy Strang (*Marabou Stork Nightmares*)

THE DIRTY DOZEN . . .

Bubbling under . . .

Renton is plagued by strange dreams wherein Gordon Hunter of Hibs and Yoko Ono scream hideous insults at him, while chewing up dismembered bodies in a neon-lit room. (*Trainspotting*)

24

COUNTER–ATTACK ON CHEAP BOOZE

A letter to the editor, originally published in *Scotland On Sunday*, November 2009:

Sir! —

I confess to permitting myself a wry chuckle on reading last week's front page headline "Irvine Welsh targets cheap booze" (News, 22nd November).

As a frequent drinking companion of the author for well over three decades, I can happily confirm for your readers that Irvine Welsh has indeed targeted cheap booze on numerous occasions, although perhaps not quite in the way your headline implied.

Indeed, this targeting has led to his direct consultation with — and subsequent temporary incarceration by — police officers on the vexing problem in question.